What Teachers
Know About Language

CAL SERIES ON LANGUAGE EDUCATION
Series Editors: Joel Gómez, Terrence G. Wiley, M. Beatriz Arias, and Joy Kreeft Peyton, *Center for Applied Linguistics, Washington, DC, USA.*

Current and aspiring education professionals need accessible, high-quality, research-based resources on language learning, instruction, and assessment. This series provides such resources, serving to inform teachers' classroom practice, enhance teacher education, and build the background knowledge of undergraduate and graduate students in applied linguistics and other language-related fields.

The books in this series explore a broad range of issues in applied linguistics and language education and are written in a style that is accessible to a broad audience, including those who are new to the field. Each book addresses a topic of relevance to those who are studying or working in the fields of language learning, language instruction, and language assessment, whether in English as a second language or other world languages. Topic areas include approaches to language instruction and assessment; approaches to content instruction and assessment for language learners; professional development for educators working with language learners; principles of second language acquisition for educators; and connections between language policy and educational practice.

All books in this series are externally peer-reviewed.

Full details of all the books in this series and of all our other publications can be found on http://www.multilingual-matters.com, or by writing to Multilingual Matters, St Nicholas House, 31-34 High Street, Bristol BS1 2AW, UK.

CAL SERIES ON LANGUAGE EDUCATION: 2

What Teachers Need to Know About Language

2nd Edition

Edited by

Carolyn Temple Adger,
Catherine E. Snow, and
Donna Christian

MULTILINGUAL MATTERS
Bristol • Blue Ridge Summit

DOI https://doi.org/10.21832/ADGER0186
Library of Congress Cataloging in Publication Data
A catalog record for this book is available from the Library of Congress.
Names: Adger, Carolyn Temple editor. | Snow, Catherine E., editor. |
    Christian, Donna editor.
Title: What Teachers Need to Know About Language/Edited by Carolyn Temple
    Adger, Catherine E. Snow, and Donna Christian.
Description: Second Edition. | Blue Ridge Summit, Pennsylvania:
    Multilingual Matters, [2018] | Series: CAL Series on Language Education:
    2 | Includes bibliographical references and index.
Identifiers: LCCN 2018005117| ISBN 9781788920179 (paperback : alk. paper) |
    ISBN 9781788920186 (hardback : alk. paper) | ISBN 9781788920193 (pdf) |
    ISBN 9781788920209 (epub) | ISBN 9781788920216 (kindle)
Subjects: LCSH: Linguistic minorities--Education--United States. | Children
    of minorities--Education--United States. | Teachers--In-service
    training--United States. | Language and education--United States.
Classification: LCC LC3728 .W43 2018 | DDC 371.102/2--dc23 LC record available at
https://lccn.loc.gov/2018005117

British Library Cataloguing in Publication Data
A catalogue entry for this book is available from the British Library.

ISBN-13: 978-1-78892-018-6 (hbk)
ISBN-13: 978-1-78892-017-9 (pbk)

Multilingual Matters
UK: St Nicholas House, 31-34 High Street, Bristol BS1 2AW, UK.
USA: NBN, Blue Ridge Summit, PA, USA.

Website: www.multilingual-matters.com
Twitter: Multi_Ling_Mat
Facebook: https://www.facebook.com/multilingualmatters
Blog: www.channelviewpublications.wordpress.com

The policy of Multilingual Matters/Channel View Publications is to use papers
that are natural, renewable, and recyclable products, made from wood grown in
sustainable forests. In the manufacturing process of our books, and to further
support our policy, preference is given to printers that have FSC and PEFC Chain of
Custody certification. The FSC and/or PEFC logos will appear on those books where
full certification has been granted to the printer concerned.

Typeset by Deanta Global Publishing Services Limited.
Printed and bound in the UK by the CPI Books Group Ltd.

Contents

Contributors

Carolyn Temple Adger is a sociolinguist and a senior fellow at the Center for Applied Linguistics, Washington, DC. She has conducted research on language use in linguistically diverse classrooms and contributed knowledge about language to educational practice in the United States and several African countries. Her most recent book is *Dialects at School: Educating Linguistically Diverse Students* (Routledge, 2017), co-authored with Christian, Reaser, and Wolfram.

Rebecca M. Alper is an assistant professor in the Communication Sciences and Disorders Department at Temple University. She completed her PhD at the University of Iowa, where she was a presidential fellow, and a postdoctoral fellowship with Kathy Hirsh-Pasek at Temple University. Dr. Alper studies the role of clinicians and caregivers as agents of early speech-language and pre-literacy intervention.

Li-Rong Lilly Cheng is professor in the School of Speech, Language, and Hearing Sciences at San Diego State University and managing director of the Confucius Institute. She is president of the International Association of Logopedics and Phoniatrics (IALP). Dr. Cheng has published numerous articles and books on language learning and language teaching focusing on the development of an optimal language learning environment.

Donna Christian is a senior fellow at the Center for Applied Linguistics. Her research focuses on the role of language in education, with a special interest in second language learning, dialect diversity, dual language education, and public policy. She is a co-author of *Dialects at School: Educating Linguistically Diverse Students* (Routledge, 2017) and editor of a special issue of the *International Multilingual Research Journal* on dual language education (2016).

Kristin Denham is director of the linguistics program and professor of linguistics in the English Department and the Linguistics Program at Western Washington University. Her publications include *Linguistics for Everyone* (Wadsworth, 2013), co-authored with Anne Lobeck; *Linguistics at School* (Cambridge, 2010), co-edited with Lobeck; articles on syntax; and articles, websites, and curriculum materials on linguistics in K-12 education.

Joanna Duggan is an associate director in the PreK-12 English Learner Education program area at the Center for Applied Linguistics. She has taught K-12 ESL in the United States and EFL in the Czech Republic and Spain, where she served in bilingual Spanish/English classrooms. Ms. Duggan holds an MSc with distinction in applied linguistics from the University of Edinburgh.

Kimberly C. Feldman is a teacher educator and PhD candidate in Language, Literacy, and Culture at the University of Maryland–Baltimore County studying exemplary teachers' negotiation of literacy theory, policy, and practice. She taught high school English in a Yupik village in Alaska and in schools near Atlanta and Baltimore. She has been a National Board Certified teacher and Howard County (MD) Teacher of the Year.

Lily Wong Fillmore, a linguist, was on the University of California Berkeley's School of Education faculty from 1974 to 2004. Much of her research, teaching, and writing over the past four and a half decades has focused on issues related to the education of language minority students. Since retiring in 2004, she has worked with educators in many urban school districts and continues to collaborate with the Council of the Great City Schools to improve academic language and literacy instruction for English learners.

Emily Phillips Galloway is an assistant professor at Vanderbilt University's Peabody College. Her work has been featured in *Reading Research Quarterly*, *Applied Psycholinguistics*, and *Reading and Writing: An Interdisciplinary Journal*. With a commitment to researcher/practitioner partnerships, she co-authored with Nonie Lesaux and Sky Marietta a recent book entitled, *Advanced Literacy Instruction in Linguistically Diverse Settings: A Guide for School Leaders*.

Daniel Ginsberg is manager of education, research, and professional development at the American Anthropological Association. Previously, he worked as a language test developer at the Center for Applied Linguistics, an ESL teacher at Malden (MA) High School, and an English language fellow in Kragujevac, Serbia. He holds a PhD in linguistics from Georgetown University and an MA in TESOL from the School for International Training.

Roberta Michnick Golinkoff is Unidel H. Rodney Sharp professor at the University of Delaware. Her work in language development, spatial learning, and play has received numerous prizes and has been funded by federal agencies. She is passionate about disseminating developmental science for improving children's and families' lives. Her latest book is *Becoming Brilliant: What Science Tells Us About Raising Successful Children* (APA Press), co-authored with Hirsh-Pasek.

Kathryn Hirsh-Pasek is the Stanley and Debra Lefkowitz faculty fellow in the Department of Psychology at Temple University and a senior fellow at the Brookings Institution. Her research examines early language and literacy development, and the role of play in learning. She is author of 14 books, hundreds of publications, and the QUILS Language Screener for children 3–6. Her awards include the American Psychological Association's Bronfenbrenner Award.

Elizabeth R. Howard is an associate professor of bilingual education in the Neag School of Education at the University of Connecticut, where she teaches graduate courses on linguistic and cultural diversity and conducts research on dual language education, biliteracy development, and the preparation of teachers to work with multilingual learners. She served as a bilingual teacher in California and Costa Rica.

Iris Kirsch has taught English in Baltimore City Public Schools for the past 11 years. She also organizes educational events with the Red Emma's Bookstore Coffeehouse collective.

Thomas H. Levine is an associate professor of curriculum and instruction at the Neag School of Education, University of Connecticut. He and Elizabeth Howard co-facilitated the faculty learning community described in their chapter. Dr. Levine has taught social studies methods for preservice teachers and led professional development about groups traditionally omitted from curricula. He and his wife are raising twin daughters to be bilingual and bicultural.

Anne Lobeck is a professor of English and Linguistics at Western Washington University, where she teaches courses on linguistics and education, and other topics. She is a long-standing member of the Linguistic Society of America's Language in the School Curriculum Committee and has worked with practicing and preservice teachers to integrate linguistics into the K-12 curriculum. She has edited two volumes on linguistics and education.

Lillian R. Masek is a graduate student in the Department of Psychology at Temple University. Her graduate work focuses on the role of caregiver/child interaction in the development of early language and school readiness skills. Ms. Masek received her master's degree from the University of Louisville, where she also taught middle school Spanish.

Lindsey A. Massoud is a senior research associate at the Center for Applied Linguistics in the PreK-12 English Learner Education program area. She conducts research and teacher professional development on sheltered instruction, technology use, language instruction and assessment, and culturally responsive instruction. She is a co-author of a CAL Practitioner Brief, *Implementing the Common Core for English Learners: Responses to Common Questions.*

Sarah C. K. Moore is program director of PreK-12 English Learner Education at the Center for Applied Linguistics, where she oversees projects addressing the educational needs of emergent bilingual students. She edited *Language Policy Processes and Consequences: Arizona Case Studies* (Multilingual Matters, 2014) and co-edited *Handbook of Heritage, Community, and Native American Languages: Research, Policy, and Practice* (Routledge, 2014).

Sonia Nieto is professor emerita of language, literacy, and culture at the University of Massachusetts, Amherst. She has devoted her professional life to issues of equity, diversity, and social justice. She is the author of 11 books and has received many awards for her scholarship and advocacy, including six honorary doctorates. In 2015, she was elected a member of the National Academy of Education.

Jeffrey Reaser is an associate professor of English at North Carolina State University where he coordinates the secondary English education program and serves as associate director of the Language and Life Project. He is co-author of the dialect awareness program, *Voices of North Carolina* (2007) and the books *Talkin' Tar Heel: How Our Voices Tell the Story of North Carolina* (2014) and *Dialects at School: Educating Linguistically Diverse Students* (2017).

Mary Schleppegrell is professor of education at the University of Michigan, Ann Arbor. A linguist, she is the author of *The Language of Schooling* (Erlbaum, 2004), *Focus on Grammar and Meaning* (with Luciana de Oliveira, Oxford University Press, 2015), and many other publications. She uses systemic functional linguistics (SFL) to explore the challenges of teaching and learning across school subjects.

Catherine Snow is the Patricia Albjerg Graham professor of education at Harvard University, with part-time visiting professor appointments at the University of Oslo and the University of Johannesburg. She has published extensively on first and second language acquisition and literacy; has chaired three National Academies of Sciences, Engineering, and Medicine committees; and is a former president of the American Educational Research Association and a member of the American Academy of Arts and Sciences, and the National Academy of Education.

Paola Uccelli is an associate professor at the Harvard Graduate School of Education (HGSE). Her research examines sociocultural and individual differences in school-relevant language development in bilingual and monolingual students in the United States and several Latin American countries. She studied linguistics at the Pontificia Universidad Católica del Perú and subsequently earned her doctoral degree in human development and psychology at HGSE.

Introduction

Carolyn Temple Adger, Catherine E. Snow,
and Donna Christian

This book represents a conversation among educators and researchers concerned with language and literacy development in today's linguistically and culturally diverse student populations. The conversation began by chance in the late 1990s at an international conference on literacy when Catherine Snow and Lily Wong Fillmore began talking about the escalating demands that the educational system in the United States places on teachers without giving them the support they need to meet those demands. Snow had just chaired a National Research Council Committee on Prevention of Reading Difficulties in Young Children that summarized what teachers would need to know to provide all children with ample and equitable opportunities to learn to read. Few of the nation's teacher education programs provided the depth and breadth of information that committee members felt was needed. Meanwhile, Fillmore had been pressing for more attention to language and literacy in teacher education and at the University of California, Berkeley, had been teaching one of the few courses in the country that addressed these issues. Clearly, the two scholars agreed, teachers need more knowledge about domains related to language and literacy than teacher education programs typically provide. They decided to develop a paper laying out their views and circulate it to colleagues for comment.

That paper—the first version of this volume's focal chapter, "What Teachers Need to Know About Language"—came to the attention of the Office of Educational Research and Improvement (OERI) in the U.S. Department of Education, who invited Snow and Fillmore to develop a workshop that would help educators think creatively about some of the issues raised there. Snow and Fillmore conducted the workshops in 1999 at three regional conferences organized by the U.S. Department of Education, focusing on how to make the challenges of language and literacy development clear, a difficult task for educators who themselves had no difficulty acquiring language and literacy skills. A composite videotape and viewer's guide, *Why Reading Is Hard*, were developed to bring the workshop to those involved in the professional development of teachers (Adger *et al.*, 2001; Clair, 2001). The paper, first published by the ERIC Clearinghouse on Languages and Linguistics (Fillmore & Snow, 2000), grounded the first edition of *What Teachers Need to Know*

1

About Language (Adger *et al.*, 2002). In that volume, the editors invited colleagues from several educational domains to comment and discuss the implications of Fillmore and Snow's arguments for their area of work. Perspectives ranged from early childhood education to teacher preparation to standards for teacher performance.

This second edition continues the conversation. How to prepare teachers to support their students' language and literacy development remains a challenge, especially since linguistic diversity continues to grow in U.S. schools (and indeed around the world). Centered on a revised, updated version of Fillmore and Snow's core chapter from the first edition, this volume adds a new set of voices to the conversation about what teachers need to know about language. All of them speak to what Fillmore and Snow have identified as central concerns about language in today's educational enterprise.

Perspectives on Teachers' Knowledge about Language

This volume begins with Fillmore and Snow's exposition on the knowledge about language that all teachers need. The authors argue that teachers need deep and broad expertise about language because of the range of functions they must serve. As communicators with students from diverse backgrounds, teachers need to understand that structural differences among languages and contrasting cultural patterns for language use may affect their students' discourse. In their role as educators, teachers need to know how English proficiency develops in native speakers and in speakers who are learning English as a second language. Understanding language development and acquisition helps teachers select appropriate materials for their students. Similarly, their role as evaluators calls for an understanding of what language behaviors to expect based on students' language backgrounds, so that predictable dialect and language learning features are not confused with language deficit or delay. Teachers are also expected to know about language by virtue of their role as educated human beings, and to contribute this information to discussions in schools and beyond. Finally, teachers are important agents of socialization, who support children's developing identities as students and who help children from a wide variety of homes and societies learn to function comfortably and successfully at school, sometimes in a new language and culture.

Building on this functional rationale, Fillmore and Snow outline what teachers should know about language by identifying questions they should be able to answer and relate to their classroom practice. The first set of questions focuses on oral language:

- What are the basic units of language?
- What's regular and what isn't? How do forms relate to each other?
- How is the lexicon acquired and structured?

- Are vernacular dialects different from "bad English" and, if so, how?
- What is academic English?
- What kind of instructional support is needed for learning English?
- Why has the acquisition of English by non-English-speaking children not been more universally successful?

The second set concerns written language:

- Why is English spelling so complicated?
- Why do some children have more trouble than others in developing early reading skills?
- What makes a sentence or a text easy or difficult to understand?
- Why do students have trouble with structuring narrative and expository writing?
- What other issues need to be considered for student writing development?

The chapter's final section suggests areas related to language that should be covered in preservice and in-service teacher learning. These topics illuminate fundamental issues in educating English learners and others who might experience problems in language and literacy learning: language and linguistics, language and cultural diversity, sociolinguistics for educators in a linguistically diverse society, language development, second language learning and teaching, the language of academic discourse, and text analysis and language understanding in educational settings.

The next three chapters target academic language, a central concern for Fillmore and Snow and one that is mentioned in other chapters as well. In Chapter 2, "Analyzing *Themes*: Knowledge About Language for Exploring Text Structure," Mary Schleppegrell expands on Fillmore and Snow's attention to academic language by describing an approach to analyzing text structure that can help students comprehend what they read and write their own texts. Teaching students to use the approach means that teachers must understand the language forms and functions it entails.

In Chapter 3, "What Educators Need to Know About Academic Language: Insights from Recent Research," Paola Uccelli and Emily Phillips Galloway define the scope of academic language, a construct that is not easily pinned down but one that educators need to understand because mastering academic language is fundamental to academic success. Their primary concern is specifying the academic language skills that all literate English speakers, especially those learning English as a second language, need to acquire and demonstrating why those skills are important. They show too how teachers can support academic language skill development.

In Chapter 4, "Language and Instruction: Research-Based Lesson Planning and Delivery for English Learner Students," Sarah C. K. Moore, Lindsey A. Massoud, and Joanna Duggan detail ways that teachers can structure lessons so that their students who are English learners can build academic language skills as they learn subject area content. To do this, teachers need to understand their students' language backgrounds, their language and literacy development, and the language demands of the lesson. All of this requires substantial knowledge about language.

Chapter 5, "'Languagizing' the Early Childhood Classroom: Supporting Children's Language Development," is by Rebecca M. Alper, Lillian R. Masek, Kathy Hirsh-Pasek, and Roberta Golinkoff. Here, we see induction into academic language, as teachers engage young children in classroom interaction on the topics and in the discourse patterns that schools value. For working with children whose language backgrounds do not match school expectations, teachers need to know how to question and otherwise invite their students to participate in the language of schooling.

In Chapter 6, "Working with Families of Diverse Backgrounds: Learning from Teachers Who 'Read' Their Students," Sonia Nieto describes the dispositions that teachers need in addition to skills and knowledge about language, particularly when they teach diverse populations. By exploring three teachers' stories, she demonstrates that knowing about each student's family and their cultural traditions, practices, and values disposes teachers to help their students' build on their funds of knowledge.

Chapter 7, "What Teachers Need to Know About Language: A Focus on Language Disorders," by Li-Rong Lilly Cheng, takes up the challenge of assessing language development in multilingual children. Cheng stresses the key role of the teacher, who must know enough about first and second language development to pick up on red flags and make referrals when they are warranted. She outlines and exemplifies a thorough diagnostic procedure involving teachers' and others' records, observation, testing, and interviews that can help practitioners distinguish difference from disorder.

Chapter 8, "What Teachers Know About Language," by Kimberly C. Feldman, Daniel Ginsberg, and Iris Kirsch, is another account of the teacher efficacy that Nieto profiles in Chapter 6, this one from teachers themselves. The authors describe ways in which they have used their knowledge about language to teach their linguistically and culturally diverse high school students about language. Here again, academic language is at the center, this time with an emphasis on the role of Standard English and other dialects.

In Chapter 9, "Language Awareness Programs: Building Students' and Teachers' Sociolinguistic Knowledge," Jeffrey Reaser reports on work that he and other sociolinguists have done that enables educators to teach students about language variation, a field in which teacher knowledge is typically thin. He argues that scientific information about dialects helps to counter language prejudice and celebrate difference, and it is fundamental to preparing teachers for serving students in a diverse society.

Chapters 10 and 11 suggest how readers might make use of this second edition, based on the authors' use of the first edition. In Chapter 10,

"Reflections on 'What Teachers Need to Know About Language (2002)'," Kristen Denham and Anne Lobeck show how they have used that first edition in introducing the essential linguistic background to their university students, who include preservice teachers. They point out that beginning in the 1960s, educators were discouraged from teaching about language structure, which resulted in generations of teachers particularly in need of linguistic education.

In the final chapter, Chapter 11, "What Teacher Educators Need to Know About Language and Language Learners: The Power of a Faculty Learning Community," Elizabeth R. Howard and Thomas H. Levine describe their faculty learning community, which was devoted to enhancing the faculty's abilities to prepare preservice teachers for linguistically diverse schools. The chapter presents the group's organizing principles and activities, with a view to encouraging other teacher education faculties to learn together and engage in change that improves their practice. Enriching faculty members' understandings about language is a practical step toward enriching teacher education, as Fillmore and Snow advocate.

Shared Foci

Several themes cut across the responses to Fillmore and Snow's chapter. All of the authors agree that deeper knowledge on the part of teachers about language, linguistics (especially sociolinguistics), and language learning and development—that is, educational linguistics—is vital to better education for U.S. students. At present, many teachers are underprepared to help their students develop the language and literacy skills they need to succeed in school and careers. Addressing issues of teacher learning remains challenging, but several chapters take them on. The final two describe approaches to deepening preservice teachers' knowledge— by including courses on linguistics in teacher preparation (Chapter 10, Denham and Lobeck) and by spreading knowledge about language across the faculty (Chapter 11, Howard and Levine). Chapter 3 (Uccelli and Phillips Galloway) urges in-service teacher training that illuminates the centrality of language in learning and gives teachers tools for supporting their students' academic language development. Chapter 9 (Reaser) shows that teachers learn with their students when more knowledgeable others step in to their classrooms.

Classroom practice

The Fillmore and Snow chapter emphasizes teacher knowledge, bringing in classroom practice by way of example. Other chapters take up practice more centrally. Schleppegrell (Chapter 2) provides examples of *Theme* analyses in several texts that students would undertake, guided by teachers. Uccelli and Phillips Galloway (Chapter 3) include a teacher's lesson planning framework for addressing academic language explicitly. Alper, Masek, Hirsh-Pasek, and Golinkoff (Chapter 5) show quite specifically what teachers can do throughout the school day to create contexts for early academic language development. Feldman, Ginsberg, and Kirsch (Chapter 8) exemplify linguistically informed teaching with lessons they taught.

Academic language

Since the first edition of *What Teachers Need to Know About Language*, understandings about the substance of academic language have grown along with instructional practices that teachers can use to promote it, due in part to the pioneering work of Schleppegrell (Chapter 2) and Uccelli (Chapter 3). Every chapter in this second edition deals in some way with academic language, at least implicitly.

Language variation

Another aspect of language in which there has been progress since the first edition regarding classroom instruction is language variation. Reaser (Chapter 9) lays out various programs for enhancing students' awareness and insight into dialect differences, including his own work. Feldman, Ginsberg, and Kirsch (Chapter 8) describe their own classroom practices for building students' respect for dialect differences and expanding their dialect choices. Still, language variation remains an urgent area to address because dialect prejudice is so prevalent and teachers' knowledge about it is typically underdeveloped.

Bilingualism

Another area in which teacher and teacher educator learning needs to advance is bilingual development. Despite the clear social, economic, and cognitive advantages of proficiency in more than one language, some still underestimate the language skills of children who are learning English as a second (or additional) language. Cheng (Chapter 7) shows what a challenge it can be for schools to evaluate and diagnose language delay in bilingual students if knowledge about language development is limited. Nieto (Chapter 6) shows what positive effects can occur when teachers prioritize understanding their students' social and cultural backgrounds, including their linguistic competence, in order to scaffold their learning.

Standards

New since the first edition are the Common Core State Standards, which figure prominently in Fillmore and Snow's chapter and which several other chapters mention as motivation for teacher learning. Because these standards represent some level of consensus, because they are tied to testing, and because standards are associated with change, they can provide an opening for enhancing teacher learning about language.

Conclusion

This edition of *What Teachers Need to Know About Language* is substantially different from the first one in two ways: The core chapter by Fillmore and Snow has been updated to reflect changing (and persistent) conditions in schools and teacher education, and an all-new assemblage of observers from different vantage points has been called on to extend and comment on the core chapter. We see this volume then as both exemplifying and advancing the important conversation about the interaction of language and learning in education—in both K-12 schools and teacher preparation programs.

References

Adger, C.T., Clair, N. and Smith, D. (2001) *Why Reading Is Hard (DVD)*. Washington, DC: Center for Applied Linguistics.

Adger, C.T., Snow, C.E. and Christian, D. (eds) (2002) *What Teachers Need to Know About Language*. Washington, DC/McHenry, IL: Center for Applied Linguistics/Delta Systems Co., Inc.

Clair, N. (2001) *Why Reading Is Hard: Viewer's Guide*. Washington, DC: Center for Applied Linguistics.

Fillmore, L.W. and Snow, C.E. (2000) *What Teachers Need to Know About Language*. Washington, DC: Center for Applied Linguistics/ERIC Clearinghouse on Languages and Linguistics. ED 444 379.

1 What Teachers Need to Know About Language

Lily Wong Fillmore and Catherine E. Snow

Prologue

A decade and a half ago, we found ourselves together at a conference at which many of the talks were given in Catalan. Unable to follow them, we withdrew to a shady spot where we started to chat about a shared concern—that many teachers had insufficient access to information about language structure, language analysis, bilingualism, and literacy to be able to optimize their instruction or maximize their contributions to discussions about language policy. In response to our concern, we sketched out the text of "What Teachers Need to Know About Language," producing in effect a long list of topics that we argued deserved more attention in teacher education and professional development. We presented those topics in the chapter that opened the previous edition of this work. We return now, some 16 years later, to the same challenge, but with the recognition that the formulation of the Common Core State Standards (CCSS) (National Governors Association, 2010), the move toward requiring students to read more complex text and to produce argumentative writing, and the persistent failure of policies for educating language minority students have made it both more urgent and more difficult.

In the meantime, though, we think the field has made considerable progress in defining, if not resolving, the challenge. For example, there is now general recognition that adolescents need ongoing instruction in reading to help them cope with the academic language and the discipline-specific discourse forms they encounter in their texts. The study of academic language, which was nascent when we wrote the first version of this chapter and which we referred to only glancingly, has now generated data, theory, tools, assessments, and instructional practices. Researchers have specified discipline-specific features of text, emphasizing that even good basic readers need to learn things about reading texts in history, science, or math that they can't learn from reading narratives.

These advances in the field present even more compelling demands for teachers to be knowledgeable about language than those we addressed when we first wrote on this topic. How might this kind of knowledge contribute to better instruction? We offer an example of linguistically informed teaching to which we will return throughout this chapter. It stands in counterpoint to efforts that respond to the need for more attention to language with explicit teaching of forms (teaching lists of academic vocabulary words, teaching about morphological derivations, teaching the discourse elements of an argument) unhinged from function. The best way to teach language forms, we contend, is to present them in text, where they display their functions, and then to explore with students what the functions are and how the forms fulfill them.

This process is demonstrated here by a teacher working with a group of five third graders who are recently arrived English learners. During this 20-minute session, the teacher takes them on a close walk through a sentence from a science text their class has been reading.

OK—so let me read this first—I'll read it twice—and after that you can read it as many times as you need to before you write down what you think this sentence is saying: *The wires behind your wall that carry electricity to lights and appliances are made of metal, usually copper.*

After reading the sentence, which is written on chart paper, the teacher hands the students some Post-it notes on which they are to jot down their initial understanding of the sentence, a relatively complex one with multiple modifiers (*behind your wall* and *that carry electricity to lights and appliances*) in its subject noun phrase. While the words are neither difficult nor especially technical, some are nonetheless unfamiliar to students who have had only a year or so of exposure to English. Over the course of this short lesson, the teacher guides the students in a deconstruction of the sentence, helping them figure out what each part means and how it relates to the other parts of the sentence.

"What's the subject of this sentence? What is this sentence about?" she asks. "About wires," a student says. The teacher nods, "This sentence is about the wires (pointing to the first two words on the chart). Now we are going to find out what the rest of the sentence is telling us about the wires." The students, guided by their teacher, work out the meaning and function of each part of the sentence, but stumble when they arrive at the word *appliances*. A student reads: "that carry electricity to lights and uh—uh-pleyshus." "Appliances," the teacher repeats. "I can tell by the fact that you had trouble saying that word that it's probably not a word you are familiar with. Does anyone know what appliances are?"

The students do not. The teacher guesses that the students might also have difficulty understanding other words that make up the sentence, even ones they read correctly. The word *appliances* presented a special challenge—it denotes a category of household equipment or devices that serves particular functions, and that, in this case, is powered by electricity. The teacher could have simply said just that and been done with defining it, or have had on hand a chart depicting such devices. But she does something far more beneficial: She engages her students in constructing a conceptual understanding of *appliances* as a categorical term. She guides them to think about devices that are powered by electricity. The students begin by suggesting buses and cell phones as examples. After distinguishing between battery power and the electrical power from the wires that the sentence tells them are behind the wall, the teacher redirects them to think about household devices that must be plugged into the wall to operate. "Computers" is the first suggestion, but when it comes to other devices, the students have difficulty naming them in English: Holding up his hands to suggest a large object, a student offers, "The—the thing that you put when you put when you're cooking?" The following exchange reveals how the teacher provides these English learners opportunities to draw on their prior knowledge to communicate their understanding in a language they are just learning:

T:	(Repeating student's utterance) "The thing that you put when you're cooking." Is it big or is it small?
S1:	It's big. (Gesturing, again hands apart indicating object about 2 feet wide)
T:	It's big, and what do you put on it?
SS:	Um, pan!
T:	Pans, good. Does anyone know the word for that big thing in the kitchen that you put pans on to cook?
SS:	uhm…
S2:	A cooker.
T:	A cooker. I'm glad you put that there because something that cooks, if you add an 'E-R' there, it is like a cookER, because I teach, and I am a teachER. So something that cooks could be a "cooker." But it has another word, so we can call it an oven, you know the word "oven"? And how about stove? Do you know the word "stove"?
S2 & SS:	(Excitedly): Oh yeah! Yeah!
T:	That's the one you were thinking about! OK! Anything else you know that runs with electricity?

The teacher goes on to elicit words for other electrically powered household devices from the students: *freezer, refrigerator, vacuum cleaner, washer, dryer*, etc. They lack the English vocabulary to name them, but she patiently draws out descriptions of their functions or what one does with them, and then she offers the English word for the device. Together, the teacher and students identify each item and as they do, she writes that word above the word *appliances* in the sentence, which they have before them on the chart paper.

This interaction reveals that even a relatively simple, relatively brief sentence can pose comprehension and processing challenges to students. What do words like *appliance* really mean? What is "behind your wall" doing in the sentence? How does this sentence signal that copper is a kind of metal? These comprehension challenges may surprise teachers, or worse, be invisible to them. In that case, they lose an opportunity to help students dig deeper into the language used in texts, learn how to navigate that language, and in the process become better speakers, readers, and writers of English. The teacher's summarization as she nears the end of her short session with the students reveals just how her sensitivity to language and her awareness of its complexities figure in the opportunities she provides for them to discover the functions of words and structures in this sample of academic discourse:

So there are many things in our homes (pointing at the items she has written above the word *appliances*) that run with electricity that are appliances, like all these things you told me: refrigerator, freezer, oven.... Those are all appliances—OK? So, (she reads, starting from the beginning of the sentence) "the wires" (circling the phrase *behind your wall*) "that are located" (pointing at the word *behind*) this is a word that tells us where—(she writes *where* above the word *behind* on the chart) "behind your wall"—(she points at the relative clause) "that carry electricity to lights and appliances" (she circles the words she has written above the word *appliances*) "all these things." (Returning to the beginning of the sentence, she summarizes) "The wires that are located there and do all of this—'carry electricity to' all these things, are made of metal."

The problem of supporting English learners in reading texts like the one they were working with in this lesson is not simply one of vocabulary. We see the teacher focusing on both new words and new structures in the context of an effort to get at meaning. She extracts student observations about the function of the elements of the sentence, rather than focusing on disembodied forms (e.g., preteaching the new vocabulary) or isolated grammatical structures (e.g., relative clause constructions or appositives).

This then, in a very large nutshell, suggests how we conceptualize the question we address in this chapter: What do teachers need to know about language to work effectively with diverse students and with the many aspects of teaching and learning in which language is a key?

What Teachers Need to Know About Language

Today's teachers need access to a wide range of information to function well in the classroom. The competencies required by the various state certification standards add up to a very long list indeed, but they constitute only a beginning. The new demands created by many states' adoption of the CCSS (National Governors Association, 2010) or other versions of college- and career-ready standards for students add to the list of what teachers need to know. Even more importantly, though, the tasks that students will face when they get to university or into the workplace require that they have developed advanced communication and literacy skills—skills they can attain only if their K-12 educational experiences have prepared them well. What do their teachers need to know about language to work effectively with all students, including ones who enter school speaking languages other than English? This is a challenge faced by teachers in schools across the nation. While English learners are most heavily concentrated in five states, with 62% of this population attending schools in California, Texas, Florida, New York, and Illinois, there is hardly a school to be found in any state where there are not at least a few English learners. These students speak many languages: Spanish is the most frequent, but home languages as typologically different as Ilocano, Mixteco, Somali, Urdu, Hmong, and Polish are also represented (Ruiz Soto *et al.*, 2015).

The U.S. teaching force is not well equipped to help these English learners or students who speak vernacular dialects of English adjust to school, learn effectively and joyfully, and achieve academic success. Too few teachers share or know about their students' cultural and linguistic backgrounds, or understand the challenges inherent in learning to speak and read Standard English. In this chapter, we argue that teachers lack this knowledge because they have not had the professional preparation they need.

These issues have been brought to the foreground by 21st-century changes in educational policy and practice, in particular the introduction of the CCSS. Society has raised by quite a few notches the educational bar that all children in the United States, including newcomers, must clear in order to complete school successfully and, ultimately, to survive in the economic and social world of today. The passage of the No Child Left Behind (NCLB) legislation in 2001 established curricular standards and introduced a system of benchmark assessments to evaluate the progress that schools and students were making toward meeting those goals. Those efforts resulted from policymakers' impatience with the apparent failure of schools to educate students adequately at each level, and they led to many changes: ending the practice of "social promotion" whereby students are passed to the next grade each year whether or not they have met academic expectations; adopting high school proficiency examinations— tests of English language and literacy and of mathematics—with high school diplomas at stake; and, perhaps most significantly, introducing disaggregated reporting guidelines, so that achievement gaps between groups of students could no longer be obscured.

The limited success of the NCLB approach to enforcing higher standards reflects several of the themes of this chapter. NCLB provided support to schools for Reading First, an effort focused on K–third-grade reading, and implicitly endorsed the idea that students reading at third-grade level at the end of third grade would proceed through the higher grades without difficulty. In effect, the theory was that later reading comprehension and learning challenges all derived from an inadequate foundation in word reading accuracy and fluency. The failure of NCLB policies to improve the reading outcomes of older students made very clear that, while word reading accuracy and fluency are necessary to successful reading, they are far from sufficient. Policymakers thus embraced the opportunity to formulate newer, broader, higher standards, and most states endorsed some version of newer, higher college- and career-ready standards. These standards shift the emphasis in literacy instruction radically—away from words toward text; from accuracy toward interpretation, evaluation, and synthesis; and from summarization toward argumentation. These shifts will undoubtedly be helpful in improving educational outcomes, but only if teachers and curriculum designers understand the demands they make on students' language skills. The reauthorization of the Elementary and Secondary Education Act by Congress in December 2015, as the Every Student Succeeds Act (ESSA), adds yet another layer of complexity to the overall picture. It requires states to have in place English language proficiency standards that cover the domains of speaking, listening, reading, and writing, and annual assessments of English proficiency aligned to those standards for English learners. It allows states greater flexibility in how they assess student progress, but it requires states to align their academic standards to credit-bearing coursework at their own public postsecondary education institutions.

Another source of pressure on K-12 educators comes from tertiary education, since successful participation in the economy is increasingly dependent on a college education (Duncan & Murnane, 2014). The restriction on the use of categories such as race and ethnicity, language background, and gender in admissions decisions in higher education raises the stakes for educators. The assumption is that all applicants will be judged strictly on their own merits and in comparison to universally applied norms. For university entrance, this means scoring at an acceptable level on standardized tests. For advancement in university, it means passing writing proficiency assessments. Increasingly in the workplace, it means being a competent user of Standard English and being fully literate (Murnane & Levy, 1996).

These policies place tremendous pressures on children to achieve the levels of language and literacy competence required to pass through the gateways to high school graduation, college admission, and a good job. As it stands now, students who arrive at school with language skills that differ from those that schools expect (language minority students, speakers of nonstandard dialects, and others) are not faring well under these pressures. Does this mean that the new standards and assessments are unreasonable? Are students not motivated or smart enough to handle the higher levels of instructional demand associated with the new standards? Do teachers lack the knowledge and skills necessary to help students? What do they need to know and be able to do in order to support their students' success? In this chapter, we will argue that teachers need a thorough understanding of how language figures in education, and for that reason they must receive systematic and intensive preparation in *educational linguistics*, a term we take to mean understanding how language works, how oral language is represented in print, how literate language differs from conversational spoken language, and how dangerously language forms are imbued with values. A thorough grounding in educational linguistics would support teachers' undertakings overall, and in particular their capacity to teach literacy skills (see Snow *et al.*, 1998) and to work with English learners (see August & Shanahan, 2008; National Academies of Science, Engineering and Medicine, 2017). If approached coherently, such preparation would also, we contend, cover many of the items on that long list of desired teacher competencies compiled from state certification standards, relating as it would to skills in assessing children, in individualizing instruction, and in respecting diversity.

We begin here by presenting a rationale for current and prospective teachers to know more about language. We then turn to a brief specification of the sorts of knowledge that teachers need. This section first discusses the requisite knowledge about the oral language skills that children bring to school, how those skills vary, and why some children have persistent difficulties achieving high levels of proficiency in spoken English and in the language forms needed for school. Then, we consider written language and the particular challenges of spelling in English and of reading and writing extended texts. There is some blurring of the oral/written distinction, of necessity, and a number of observations apply to both. The final section of this chapter specifies target domains for teacher learning as input to designing an integrated, in-depth, preservice or professional development program.

Why Do Teachers Need to Know More About Language?

We distinguish five functions for which prospective educators need to know more about language than they may currently have the chance to acquire:

- teacher as communicator;
- teacher as educator;
- teacher as evaluator;
- teacher as educated human being;
- teacher as agent of socialization.

Teacher as communicator

Clearly, communication with students is essential in effective teaching. To communicate successfully, teachers must know how to structure their own language output for maximum clarity. They must also have strategies for understanding what students are saying, because understanding student talk is key to an analysis of what students know, how they understand, and what teaching moves would be useful. The dramatic demographic transformation over the past decade so that "minorities" now outnumber the white students who were once the majority (Kent, 2015) has resulted in increasingly diverse classrooms, and teachers are more likely than before to encounter students with whom they do not share a first language or dialect nor a native culture. An understanding of linguistics can help teachers see that the discourse patterns they value are aspects of their own cultures and backgrounds; they are neither universal nor inherently more valid than other possible patterns. Without such an understanding, teachers sometimes assume that there is something wrong with students whose ways of using language are not what they expect. Smitherman (1977) relates a poignant example of how teachers who do not recognize the validity of other ways of speaking can undermine their students' confidence in their own communicative abilities:

> Student (excitedly): Miz Jones, you remember that show you tole us about? Well, me and my momma 'nem—
>
> Teacher (interrupting with a "warm" smile): Bernadette, start again. I'm sorry, but I can't understand you.
>
> Student (confused): Well, it was that show, me and my momma—
>
> Teacher (interrupting again, still with that "warm" smile): Sorry, I still can't understand you.
>
> (Student, now silent, even more confused than ever, looks at floor, says nothing.)
>
> Teacher: Now Bernadette, first of all, it's *Mrs.* Jones, not *Miz* Jones. And you know it was an *exhibit*, not a *show*. Now, haven't I explained to the class over and over again that you always put yourself last when you are talking about a group of people and yourself doing something? So, therefore, you should say what?
>
> Student: My momma and me—
>
> Teacher (exasperated): No! My mother and I. Now start again, this time right.
>
> Student: Aw, that's okay, it wasn't nothin.
>
> (Smitherman, 1977: 217–218)

Studies of discourse patterns in the homes and communities of American Indians (Philips, 1993), Alaskan Natives (Wyman, 2012),

Native Hawaiians (Tharp *et al.*, 2007), Mexican Americans (Reyes & Moll, 2008; Schecter & Bayley, 2002), Puerto Ricans (Zentella, 1997), and African Americans (Heath, 1983; Meier, 2008) have shown that the speech patterns that children bring to school from their homes can be quite different from the ones that are valued at school. Acquiring the academic discourse patterns of school is an important part of the educational development of all students, but it is neither necessary nor desirable to promote this ability at the expense of the language patterns that children have already mastered and that are essential to functioning effectively in their home communities. In fact, Mrs. Jones' pedagogical approach to language development is more likely to sour children like Bernadette to the whole experience of schooling than it is to instruct them. While classroom discourse patterns are hardly invariant, there are nonetheless conventional expectations for speech behavior, which children need to learn and observe if they are to participate successfully in the social world of the classroom. It takes time, patience, and understanding on the part of teachers to inculcate school-appropriate practices in children. Noting occasions on which students appear confused or unable to abide by school discourse conventions provides clues about differences in default communication patterns and specifies where students need more guidance about how "school talk" works.

In as diverse a society as ours, teachers must be prepared to work with children from many different cultural, social, and linguistic backgrounds, whose educational needs are both varied and complex. Among them are the children of recent immigrants and refugees who arrive at school with linguistic and cultural resources that their teachers may not recognize or appreciate immediately. Some may be dealing with stress related to prior experiences and present circumstances. Teachers require an abundance of professional preparation to work effectively with students for whom the American classroom presents daunting and often puzzling experiences, students who must quickly and efficiently learn a new language in addition to curricular content. Understanding the course of second language acquisition, including such matters as the sorts of mistakes that English learners are likely to make and how much progress can be expected in a unit of time, helps teachers communicate with these students more effectively and establish realistic expectations. When communicating with English learners, it might be tempting to offer corrective feedback. But such supportive efforts might make learners self-conscious and result in derailing their communication efforts. Perhaps the kindest, gentlest way to provide helpful feedback is to adopt the practice followed by caregivers of very young children— repeating a learner's utterance along with a subtle correction of form or modification of structure. An example appears in the following excerpt from the lesson featured in the prologue, in which the teacher is asking students to explain the use of a comma separating a noun and an appositive noun phrase:

T: So why is this comma here?
S: To tell what it, what *is* it?
T: To tell—OK, you're right. To tell what *it is*.

The teacher interrupted her repetition of the student's utterance with an acknowledgment of the response as being correct, and then continued, stressing "*it is*" to draw attention to the correct order of subject and verb in the *what*-complement clause. Even advanced speakers of English as a second language (ESL) may use narrative organization or conversational patterns that differ from those of the mainstream. Understanding how their language use might differ is crucial for effective teaching. In their function as interlocutors, teachers need to know something about educational linguistics.

Teacher as educator

Teachers are responsible for selecting educational materials and activities at the right level and of the right type for all of the children in their classes. This requires that they have the expertise to assess student accomplishments and the capacity to distinguish between imperfect knowledge of English and cognitive obstacles to learning. In order to teach effectively, teachers need to know which language problems will resolve themselves with time and which need attention and intervention. In other words, they need to know a great deal about language development.

Language is a vital developmental domain throughout the years of schooling, whatever the child's linguistic, cultural, or social background. Textbooks on child development often claim that by age five or six, children have already mastered the grammar of their native language and that although they expand their vocabularies in school and add literacy skills, for the most part children have acquired language before they go to school. Such a characterization of language development is far from accurate. All children have a long way to go developmentally before they can function as mature members of their speech communities (Hoyle & Adger, 1998; Menyuk & Brisk, 2005).

The most obvious aspects of language development during the school years relate to learning to read and write. When children learn to read, they are exposed to a collection of linguistic structures, forms, and devices that they are unlikely to encounter in everyday social discourse whether in or out of school. In the process of becoming literate, children acquire the language needed for the disciplined, precise, and complex ways of expressing ideas required for mature communication. Structures and forms that emerge early take time to master. Berman (2004) has found that aspects of lexical understanding and constructions such as the passive are not mastered until adolescence because of the complex linguistic knowledge involved in their use. Control over the language of written discourse, such as inter-sentential and discourse links and the expression of multiple perspectives in academic writing, also appear to be late developments, reflecting the impact of advanced literacy, according to Tolchinsky (2004).

Teachers play a critical role in supporting language development through literacy. Beyond teaching children to read and write, they can help children learn and use aspects of language associated with the academic discourse of the various school subjects. They can help them become more aware of how language functions in various modes of communication across the curriculum. They need to understand how language works well enough to select materials that will expand their students' linguistic horizons and to plan instructional activities that give students opportunities to use the new forms and modes of expression to which they are being exposed. Teachers need to understand how to design the classroom language environment so as to optimize language and literacy learning and to avoid linguistic obstacles to content area learning. A basic knowledge of educational linguistics is a prerequisite to promoting language development with the full array of students in today's classrooms.

Teacher as evaluator

Teachers' judgments can have enormous consequences for children's lives, from the daily responses that affect students' sense of themselves as learners to the more weighty decisions about reading group placement, promotion to the next grade, or referral for evaluation. American school culture is greatly concerned with individual differences in learning ability, and judgments about ability are often based on teacher evaluations of children's language. American educators take seriously the idea that people differ in abilities and aptitudes, and they believe that such differences require differentiated treatment in school. A lot of attention is given to sorting children by ability as early as possible. Children entering kindergarten are given readiness tests to determine which of them meet the developmental expectations of school and which do not. Some schools have developmental or junior kindergartens for children who are judged not quite ready for school based on their performance on these readiness tests. In many kindergartens, children are grouped for instruction according to the notion of ability on the basis of such tests or by informal assessments of student behaviors. If they are not grouped in this way in kindergarten, they certainly are by first grade, with children sorted globally into differentiated learning groups before they have had an opportunity to discover what school is all about. Once sorted this way, children typically receive substantially different instructional treatment and materials, reinforcing any initial differences among them in speed of learning and eagerness to learn. Ones who are placed in high-ability reading groups receive the kind of instruction likely to promote enthusiastic engagement in reading. Those who are placed in lower-ability groups receive instruction focused almost exclusively on skill development, which is deemed essential for struggling learners. Unfortunately, children in lower-ability tracks learn substantially less, as documented by research on the impact of such grouping practices on academic achievement in African American and Hispanic students in elementary school (Lleras & Rangel, 2009).

Ability grouping was largely abandoned in the 1990s, in large part because of studies such as Jeannie Oakes' influential 1985 report documenting the impact of tracking practices in perpetuating inequalities in educational outcomes across student groups (Oakes, 1985). But a recent study by Loveless (2013) for the Brown Center at the Brookings Institution reports a worrisome revival of these practices, particularly in reading and math instruction. These days, grouping tends to be characterized as differentiated instruction and justified as a necessary recognition that because students have diverse needs, teachers must adjust their methods and materials to meet their needs. Differentiated instruction is especially common in classes with English learners, given their likely variability in language proficiency. The use of leveled readers is a common practice—but it is one that requires careful consideration. English learners may require somewhat simpler texts for a time, especially for independent reading, but not as main texts. The problem lies in the function that texts play in providing opportunities for learning the linguistic forms, structures, and devices characteristic of written discourse. These aspects of language are usually avoided in texts designed for students who are thought not to be ready for grade-level materials, whether because of underdeveloped language or reading skills. What students actually need is instructional support so that they can handle grade-level appropriate materials—precisely what the English learners in the group lesson featured in the prologue were receiving.

We do not mean to suggest here that children should never be sorted for any purpose. It is very effective for teachers to form small groups of children who need more time with particular instructional foci (e.g., vocabulary enrichment or long vowel spellings). It can also be helpful to group children who read at a similar level so they can discuss their books with one another. But the key to such grouping is that it be targeted (i.e., used for particular instructional purpose), flexible (i.e., as soon as individual children have acquired the targeted skill they leave that group), and objective (i.e., based on well-specified criteria directly related to the instructional target, not on global measures of readiness).

A serious worry about global tracking decisions is the questionable validity of the assessment evidence on which these placement decisions are made. Judgments of children's language and social behaviors can figure into these assessments, as can their parents' socioeconomic circumstances, factors that should not affect academic placement. Consider, for example, the uncritical reactions by many educators to public discussion of the "30-million-word gap" between children in welfare families and those in affluent families in the amount of language heard before kindergarten. The study documenting the gap was conducted in the 1970s by Hart and Risley (1995), and reflected the concern with social class differences in academic outcomes of that era (Bereiter & Englemann, 1966; Bernstein, 1971). The researchers collected an hour-long speech sample each week over a period of two years from 42 Kansas City families in their homes: 13 were higher socioeconomic status (SES) families (1 Black, 12 White); 10 middle SES (3 Black, 7 White); 13 lower SES (7 Black, 6 White); and 6 welfare (all Black). The number of words spoken by adults in the hearing of children was tallied up and compared across groups. The researchers found that high SES children heard a good many more words than did lower SES children, with the greatest difference occurring when high SES children were compared to the children in the six welfare families. Extrapolating from those findings, researchers estimated that by age three, the children of welfare parents have heard 30 million fewer words than have the children of upper SES parents, a finding they associated with the much smaller working vocabularies of the children in welfare-dependent families (500 words versus 1000). They argued that the children's vocabularies accounted for patterns of social class-related inequality in reading outcomes.

Public concern about this gap was revived in the first decade of the current millennium, sparked in part by Hart and Risley's (2003) second book, with its characterization of the stark social class differences as an "early catastrophe." Though some have criticized the Hart and Risley findings as based on small samples, as ignoring variability within social class groups, and as blind to the social and cultural influences leading to the differences observed (e.g., Avineri et al., 2016; Michaels, 2013; Miller & Sperry, 2012), there is little disagreement with the general conclusion that some children experience greater continuity between the language experiences and expectations of home and school than others. However, a lack of understanding of forces that account for differences in young children's language environments has led to simplistic responses (telling parents just to talk more, focusing on vocabulary instruction unlinked to content in early childhood classrooms) that are unlikely to be effective. It is incumbent on teachers to understand differences in children's language development so as to address them in productive ways and avoid taking them as a basis for projections of academic failure (Snow, 2017).

This brings us back to the role played by teachers as evaluators. Guided by a readiness checklist, kindergarten and first-grade teachers answer questions like the following about the children in their classes: Do they know their first and last name? Can they follow simple instructions? Can they ask questions? Can they answer them? Do they know the names of the colors in their crayon boxes? Can they produce short narratives? Do they know their mother's name? Can they count to 10? The assumption is that all children at age five or six should have the specific abilities that are assessed, and anyone who does not is not ready for school. In reality, such abilities and skills are hardly universal nor are they indicative of learning ability. For example, there are cultures in which children are not told what their mother's name is, and if a child were somehow to learn it, he/she would never speak it or acknowledge that he/she had such information. In Wong Fillmore's traditional Chinese culture, this was true, but it has changed in modern Chinese culture, especially among Chinese immigrants in America. There are rather great differences across cultures in the kinds of linguistic accomplishments believed to be appropriate for children at any age. The kinds of skills that children bring from home reflect those differences in belief. In some cultures, for example, children are encouraged to listen rather than to ask questions of adults. Only rude and poorly reared children would chatter away in the presence of an authority figure like the teacher. When children do not perform as expected on a test, it does not necessarily mean that they are lacking in ability—particularly if they do not know the language in which the questions were asked. Given the diversity in our society, it is imperative to recognize that young children may differ considerably in their inventory of skills and abilities, and these differences should not be treated as reflecting deficiencies in ability.

To make valid judgments about students' abilities, teachers also need to understand the different sources of variation in language use—whether a particular pattern signals membership in a language community that speaks a vernacular variety of English, normal progress for a second language learner of English, normal deviations from the adult standard that are associated with earlier stages of development, or developmental delay or disorder. The challenge of making appropriate special education placements is compounded by the fact that normal language features associated with a vernacular variety of English or with learning English as a second language may be misinterpreted as an indication of developmental delay (Artiles et al., 2005; Linn & Hemmer, 2011; Sullivan, 2011). The odds of English learners being referred and placed in special education were found to be 70% higher than for non-English learners in one school district, principally because they had difficulty speaking English, a language they were in the process of learning (Hehir & Mosqueda, 2007). The high percentage of special education referrals for English learners and vernacular dialect speakers may simply reflect teachers' strategies for getting these children extra help, often from a speech-language pathologist who is relatively well trained in language development issues. But if teachers knew more about language, they could institute instructional processes to address these children's needs without the risks inherent in labeling children.

Considering the potential harm of misconstruing children's language use, investing in educational linguistic training about the course of language development and about language variation seems a wise use of teacher preparation resources.

Teacher as educated human being

Teachers need to have access to basic information about language for the same reasons that any educated member of society should know something about language. Understanding the basics of how one's own language works contributes to proficient reading and writing. Recognizing the difference between nouns and verbs, consonants and vowels, or oral and literate forms is as basic for the liberally educated human being as is knowledge about addition and subtraction, nutrition, or the solar system. Students educated in the United States should also know something about the differences between the structure of English and that of other languages just as surely as they should know about the tripartite organization of the U.S. government. It used to be the case that English grammar was taught to students beginning in about the fifth grade and continuing through eighth grade in what was then called grammar school. Such instruction was largely discontinued in the 1960s, leading to the decline in general knowledge about grammar for most adults. Parochial schools continued teaching grammar for several decades, and for adults who attended such schools, grammar is remembered, whether fondly or otherwise, primarily as exercises in sentence diagramming. For most teachers, any direct exposure to grammar has come from foreign language courses. Thus, teachers who have taken Spanish may know something about verb conjugations and perhaps remember arcane facts about which of the two forms corresponding to English "be," *ser* or *estar*, should be used in various situations.

Recent changes to English language arts curricular frameworks and standards call for greater attention to grammar in the context of writing, if not as a subject worthy of study on its own merit. The CCSS, for example, call for students to demonstrate a command of Standard English grammar and usage when speaking and writing. Thus, grammar is finding its way back into the school's curriculum, and teachers will find themselves teaching it in English language arts across the grades.

Teachers who have not had the opportunity to study the structure of English or to learn another language may not feel very confident talking about language. English is the language of society; it is the language that most teachers use exclusively in their teaching; and it is the language that many teachers teach about to some extent. But how much do they know about it? Do they know its history? Do they know what languages are related to it? Do they know why there are so many peculiar spellings in English? Do they know how the language has changed over time and the effects of the printing press on change? Do they know how regional dialects develop? Teachers have practical, professional reasons to know these things, but we suggest that the attention to grammar and rhetoric that was characteristic of the lower level of a classical education was neither premature nor exaggerated. All of us should understand such matters, and we will not learn them unless teachers understand them first.

Throughout the United States, there is a real need for research-based knowledge about language teaching, language learning, and the functions of language in education. We need educational leadership to ensure that this knowledge is widely shared. Our society has had long experience with linguistic diversity, although it has never regarded that diversity as an asset to be valued and protected. The many languages spoken by American Natives and the languages of the many groups that have immigrated to the United States have been suppressed, systematically at some periods, by default at others. One venue for this process has been the school, as children become speakers of English, all too often at the cost of the language of their homes and families. In the past half-century, we have come to recognize that, while this assimilation process has worked for many, it has proven harmful for others. Bilingual education, in which children's home languages were used for instruction part of the time in school, was promulgated as a kinder, gentler way to facilitate their transition into English. It flourished for a time, but proved to be a lightning rod, attracting the wrath of those who believed that there is only room for one language in our society. A number of states and local school districts opted for "English-only" instruction for English learners. The movement to suppress bilingual education, despite its benefits for the many children served and its potential for creating a more inclusive society, experienced a major success at the turn of the millennium. In 1998, voters in California passed a public referendum aimed at banning bilingual education for the state's 1.4 million English learners. In fact, because of a constant barrage of criticism against this approach, fewer than 30% of the English learners in California were in bilingual programs at the time; but the state's voters were persuaded by arguments based on a mixture of myth (e.g., children can learn English in just one year in structured English immersion programs), worries about national unity, and misrepresentations of bilingual education programs (e.g., claims that they teach children exclusively in their home languages). California's ban on bilingual education was repealed, again by referendum, in 2016, but even tougher versions of the ban passed in Arizona and Massachusetts, essentially eliminating bilingual education as an instructional approach. The Arizona ban remains in effect, and the negative effects of the 15-year-long ban in Massachusetts are still visible. Public discussion of these propositions revealed a dismaying lack of understanding about the facts of second language learning and the nature of bilingual education. For example, cases of poorly implemented bilingual education programs were cited in support of the movement to outlaw the approach. Of course, any program can be well or badly implemented—we certainly have not outlawed teaching algebra in eighth or ninth grade because some teachers don't do it well!

Though public reaction to bilingual education is a notable case of the civic need for language knowledge, many such examples could be cited. Decisions about the use of nonstandard English forms in the classroom, about the impact of text messaging on spelling, about the appropriateness of considering rap lyrics in literature classes, about the acceptability of gender-free language, and many other such language-related topics require some sophistication in our understanding of how language works. Finally, when school districts and parent groups respond to low student performance on reading tests by turning to inappropriate methods for teaching reading or when they abandon sound methods for teaching English in the face of disappointing language achievement scores, we see the consequences of too little basic knowledge about language and literacy. Teachers are in the best position to raise the level of such discussions by adding information about language issues and promising research-based interventions.

Teacher as agent of socialization

Teachers play a unique role as agents of socialization—the process by which individuals learn the everyday practices, the system of values and beliefs, and the means and manners of communication in their cultural communities. Socialization begins in the home and continues at school. When the cultures of home and school match, the process is generally continuous: Building on what they have acquired at home from family members, children become socialized into the ways of thinking and behaving that characterize educated individuals. They learn to think critically about ideas, phenomena, and experiences; and they add the modes and structures of academic discourse to their language skills. But when there is a mismatch between the cultures of home and school, the process can be disrupted. We have discussed some ways in which mismatches between teachers' expectations of how children should behave communicatively and how they actually do behave can affect teachers' ability to assess the children's abilities and teach them effectively. In fact, what teachers say and do can determine how successfully children make the crucial transition from home to school. It can determine whether children move successfully into the world of the school and larger society as fully participating members or get shunted onto sidetracks that distance them from family, society, and the world of learning.

For many children, teachers are the first contact with the culture of the social world outside of the home. From association with family members, children have acquired a sense of who they are, what they can do, what they should value, how they should relate to the world around them, and how they should communicate. These understandings are cultural—they differ from group to group and even within groups. Children of immigrants and native-born American children from non-majority backgrounds may encounter a stark disjunction between their cultural understandings and those of the school. For example, Mexican children generally have a sure sense of self within the world of the home. The center of this universe is not the individual but the family itself. Each member is responsible for maintaining, supporting, and strengthening the family; its needs come before the needs of any individual (Valdés, 1996); the activities of the family provide children with opportunities to gain the tools and skills required for competent participation in the world of the home (Fuller & García Coll, 2010; Moreno & Pérez-Granados, 2002). For Pueblo Indian children, the central unit is the community, and its needs and requirements take precedence over those of the individual (Romero-Little, 2004). Popovi Da, a Pueblo leader, explained that

> Each person in Indian [Pueblo] society is born into his place in the community, which brings with it duties and responsibilities which he must perform throughout his life. Each member ... has an important part to play in the organization of the tribe ... putting the good of the group above his own desires. (Popovi Da, 1969)

This emphasis on community is characteristic of most American Indian groups. For children, it means shared responsibility for getting work done rather than personal endeavor and achievement.

When children from these cultures begin school, they encounter a culture that has a very different focus, one that emphasizes the primacy of the individual and considers family, group, and community needs subsidiary to individual needs. They soon discover that the school culture takes precedence over the home culture. Administrators and teachers do not accept as excuses for school absence the need to care for younger siblings when the mother is sick or to participate in a religious ritual in the community. Children learn that at school, work and progress are regarded as individual endeavors, and they are rewarded for their ability to work independently.

In the area of language and communication, children who enter school with no English are expected to learn the language of instruction as quickly as possible, often with minimal help. Children discover very quickly that the way to gain access to the social or academic world of school is by learning the language spoken there. The messages that may be conveyed to them and their parents are that the home language has no value or role in school if it is not English, and that parents who want to help their children learn English should switch to English for communication at home, read books with them in English, and in general prioritize the school language over the home language. For parents who know and speak English, this is not difficult (though it may be undesirable); for parents who do not know English well or at all, it is tantamount to telling them that they have nothing to contribute to the education of their children. Rodriguez (1982) offers a revealing account of what happens when parents are advised to switch to a language they do not speak easily or well, for the sake of their children. He describes how the lively chatter at dinnertime turned silent and how the silences in his home grew as his parents withdrew from participation in the lives of the children after teachers told them that using Spanish in the home was preventing the children from learning English.

The process of socialization into the culture of the school need not be detrimental either to the child or to the family, even when there are substantial differences between the cultures of the home and school. When teachers realize just how traumatic such an assimilation process can be for immigrant and native-born children from non-majority backgrounds, given the adjustments and accommodations they must make as they move from home to school, they can ease the process considerably. If teachers respect their students' home languages and cultures and understand the crucial role they play in the lives of the children and their families, they can help children make the necessary transitions in ways that do not undercut the role that parents and families must continue to play in their education and development. This point is well illustrated by Wong (1989) in her remarkable autobiography (first published in 1945) where she describes how teachers, from elementary school through college, helped her find her way and her voice as an American scholar, writer, and artist without forfeiting her Chinese language and culture.

What Should Classroom Teachers Know About Language?

In this section, we outline a set of questions that the average classroom teacher should be able to answer, and we identify topics that teachers and other educators should have knowledge of. We have organized them according to oral and written language domains to underscore these essential categories, even though many of the questions pertain to both domains. We focus first on oral language, then on written language. These questions and topics are not arcane or highly technical. We are certainly not proposing that all educators need to understand the range of theoretical concepts that are of interest to the professional linguist. Rather, we are identifying issues of language use in daily life, issues that require only a basic understanding of the descriptive work that linguists engage in and the concepts that they use. Decisions about how to segment the information we call for—that is, how to distribute it over preservice courses and in-service learning—and how to ensure that it will be acquired go well beyond our brief. We simply provide a (no doubt incomplete) listing of issues and a brief justification for the relevance to classroom practice of each, in the hope that those with greater expertise in teacher education and professional development can think about how to make this knowledge available to classroom practitioners.

Attention to educational linguistics might be assumed to be of particular importance to the educator specialized in dealing with language learners—the bilingual or ESL teacher. We certainly agree that prospective ESL and bilingual teachers would benefit from intensive and coherent preparation in educational linguistics. But we contend that such preparation is equally important for all classroom practitioners and, indeed, for administrators and educational researchers—though of course the specifics of more advanced preparation will vary for these groups. Expertise on language issues related to teaching and learning is important for all educators, increasingly so as the percentage of English learners and speakers of vernacular dialects grows among American students.

Oral language

We begin by attending to oral language because in their native language (and often also in a second language), children develop oral proficiency first. Oral language functions as a foundation for literacy and as the means of learning in school and out. However, despite its importance for learning, many teachers know much less about oral language than they need to know.

What are the basic units of language?

Spoken language is composed of units of different sizes: sounds (called phonemes if they function to signal different meanings in the language), morphemes (sequences of sounds that form the smallest units of meaning in a language), words (consisting of one or more morphemes), phrases (grammatically related group of words), clauses (a verb and its related arguments), sentences, and discourses. Crucial to an understanding of how language works is the idea of *arbitrariness*. Sequences of sounds have no meaning by themselves; it is only by convention that meanings are attached to sound. In another language, a sequence of sounds that is meaningful in English may mean nothing at all or something quite different.

Furthermore, each language has an inventory of phonemes that may differ from that of other languages. Phonemes can be identified by virtue of whether a change in sound makes a difference in meaning. Thus, in English *ban* and *van* constitute two different words, showing that /b/ and /v/ are different phonemes. Similarly, *fit* and *feet* are two different words, showing that the short vowel sound /I/ of *fit* is different from the long vowel sound /i/ of *feet*. In Spanish, of course, the differences between /b/ and /v/ and between /I/ and /i/ do not make a difference in meaning. Native Spanish speakers may be influenced by the phonemic inventory of Spanish when they are speaking English. They might say either *very good* or *bery good* to mean the same thing. Similarly, they may find it difficult to distinguish *hit it* from *heat it*. Dialects of English show different phonemic patterns as well. In southern U.S. varieties, for example, the vowels in *pin* and *pen* sound the same, but in northern varieties they are different. It is clear that such contrasting phonemic patterns across languages and dialects can have an impact on what words children understand, how they pronounce words, and also how they might be inclined to spell them.

The morpheme is the smallest unit of language that expresses a distinct meaning. A morpheme can be an independent or free unit, like *jump*, *dog*, or *happy*, or it can be a prefix or suffix attached to another morpheme to modify its meaning, such as *−ed* or *−ing* for verbs (*jumped*, *jumping*), plural *−s* or possessive *−s* for nouns (*dogs*, *dog's*), or *−ly* or *−ness* added to adjectives to turn them into adverbs or nouns (*happily*, *happiness*). In other words, *jumped* is a single word that contains two morphemes, *jump* and *−ed*. Units like *−ed* or *−ly* are called bound morphemes because they do not occur alone. The relevance of bound morphemes to teachers' understanding emerges most strongly in the domain of spelling, discussed below. But it is worth noting here that English, reflecting its origin as a Germanic language, features many irregular forms (see Pinker, 1999) that can cause problems. Children may produce ungrammatical forms using regular morpheme combinations, such as past tense *bringed* and plural *mans*. And just as it is informative to study contrasts in phoneme patterns across dialects, teachers should also be aware of dialect variation in morpheme combinations. For example, in African American Vernacular English, the plural form of *man* can be *mens*.

Teachers need to understand that grammatical units such as bound and free morphemes, words, phrases, and clauses operate quite differently across languages. The locative meanings expressed by prepositions such as *in*, *on*, and *between* in English are expressed by noun endings (bound morphemes) in Hungarian and are often incorporated into the structure of the verb in Korean. In Chinese, plurality and past tense are typically expressed by separate words such as *several* and *already* rather than bound morphemes (*-s* and *−ed*), but these words may be omitted if the meanings are obvious in context. The native Chinese speaker who treats plurals and past tenses as optional rather than obligatory in English is reflecting the rules of Chinese. Of course, such a student needs to learn how to produce grammatical English sentences. But understanding the variety of structures that different languages and dialects use to show meaning, including grammatical meaning such as plurality or past tense, can help teachers see the logic behind the errors of students who are learning English. When two-year-olds produce forms like *I swinged already*, we consider it charming; we need to see that the errors of older second language speakers reflect the same level of insight into the rules of the language and creativity in resolving communicative challenges.

Finally, teachers need knowledge about the larger units of language use—sentence and discourse structure—that are fundamental to understanding the unique features of academic language. We have pointed out that teachers' expectations for students' participation in classroom talk may be based on their own cultural patterns. Such simple rhetorical tasks as responding to questions require making a hypothesis about why the question is being asked and how it fits into a set of social relationships that may be specific to a culture. *Can you open the door?* might be a question about physical strength or about psychological willingness, or it might be a request. If a child gives a puzzling response to a question, the teacher who knows something about crosslinguistic differences in the rules for asking questions and making requests might well be able to analyze its source. It is critical that interpretations of language use as reflecting politeness, intelligence, or other judgments about the student be informed by this understanding of language differences.

Trouble can occur at the discourse level when students do not understand teachers' expectations about academic discourse patterns that the teachers themselves learned in school. For example, in the interactive structure typical of direct instruction, the teacher initiates an interaction, often by asking a question; a student responds; and the teacher provides feedback. But sometimes the teacher calls on another student in the third slot instead of giving feedback overtly. This move functions as repeating the same question to that student. Students need to understand variation in this fundamental classroom structure: Implicit norms for language use are part of what it means to know a language well. When teachers have explicit knowledge of rhetorical structures, they have the tools for helping children understand the expectations associated with school English.

What's regular and what isn't? How do forms relate to each other?

By virtue of being proficient English speakers and effortless readers, most adults take for granted language irregularities that can be enormously puzzling to younger and less fluent learners. Is there any difference between *dived* and *dove*? Can one similarly say both *weaved* and *wove*? Why do we say *embarrassment*, *shyness*, *likeliness*, and *likelihood*, not *embarrassness* or *embarrasshood*, *shyment*, *shyhood*, or *likeliment*? Such questions may seem odd, but they arise naturally during children's language development. Answers lie in the principles of word formation rooted in the history of English.

An important part of acquiring a vocabulary suitable for academic contexts is learning how to parse newly encountered words into their component parts, rather than simply treating complex words as long words. In many cases, the context in which a word is used and the recognition of familiar morphemes assist in interpreting and remembering words. There are probably thousands of words that most people learn in context without help, for example, *disinherit*, *pre-established*, and *decaffeinated*. The key here is that there are regular patterns for how word parts (morphemes) can be combined into longer words.

When teachers are aware of the principles of word formation in English, they can use this knowledge to aid their students in vocabulary acquisition. They should be aware, for example, of such patterns as the *d/s* alternation in pairs of related words like *evade* and *evasive*, *conclude* and *conclusive*: When they know this principle, students can learn two new words at once. Teachers should know about certain accent-placement regularities involving the suffixes written *-y* and *-ic*, so that they can help students learn groups of words together: for example, *SYNonym*, *syNONymy*, *synoNYMic*; *PHOtograph*, *phoTOGraphy*, *photoGRAPHic*; *ANalog*, *aNALogy*, *anaLOGic*; and so on. A mastery of the connections between the patterns of word formation and the rhythms of English speech equips teachers to point out such patterns in academic language and enhance students' vocabulary growth.

Spanish-speaking children can be taught to use correlated morphological structures in Spanish and English to understand sophisticated English lexical items and to expand their English vocabularies. Consider the advantages for Spanish speakers who discover that a Spanish noun that ends in *-idad* almost always has an English cognate that ends in *-ity* (*natividad* and *nativity*, *pomposidad* and *pomposity*, *curiosidad* and *curiosity*) or that nouns ending in *-idumbre* relate to nouns ending in *-itude* (*certidumbre* and *certitude*, *servidumbre* and *servitude*). If they already know the Spanish words, the parallel to English can be pointed out; if they do not know the word in either language, the parallel Spanish and English words can be taught together.

Students who come to English as native speakers of other Indo-European languages may find it helpful to be aware of the international vocabulary of science and technology (e.g., *photosynthesis* is *fotosíntesis* in Spanish, *fotosintez* in Russian; *computer* is *computador* or *computadora* in Spanish, компьютер in Russian). This could involve learning basic correspondences, the notion of cognate and how to distinguish cognates from false cognates and loanwords, enough about the history of English to be able to judge whether an English word is likely to have a cognate in the student's first language, and crosslinguistic comparisons. In order to teach these matters, teachers must understand them deeply and know how to support their students' explorations when the teacher does not know the other language involved.

How is the lexicon acquired and structured?

Almost every classroom teacher recognizes the need to teach vocabulary (the lexicon), and most teachers do so. Usually, technical or unusual words used in texts are targeted for instruction. Definitions may be solicited from the students or supplied by the teacher before the text is read in interactions along these lines:

Teacher: *Digestion*: Who knows what *digestion* means?

Student: I know, I know. When you eat.

Teacher: That's right! When we eat, we digest our food. That's *digestion*!

Often, the definitions given are rather superficial and sometimes even misleading, as in this example. Technically, the definition offered here would work better for *ingestion* than for *digestion*. Presumably, the text itself and the ensuing class discussion would clarify the meaning of *digestion*, but the initial instructional effort probably added little to the children's understanding. It takes many encounters with a word in meaningful contexts for students to acquire it (Beck *et al.*, 2002).

What does it mean to acquire a word? What do we know when we know a word? Knowing a word involves knowing something of its core meaning. In the case of *digestion*, the core meaning is the process by which the food one eats is converted into simpler forms that the body can use for energy. But few words are unidimensional in meaning or use, so knowing a word goes well beyond knowing a definition of it. Knowing a word also requires an understanding of how it relates to similar forms (e.g., *digestion, digest, ingest, digestive, indigestion*), how it can be used grammatically (i.e., its word class and the grammatical constructions it can be used in), and how it relates to other words and concepts (e.g., *food, nutrient, stomach, digestive juices, esophagus, intestines, digesting facts, Reader's Digest*). Vocabulary instruction could be more effective if teachers understood how words are learned in noninstructional contexts, through conversational interactions, and through encounters with written language. Knowing individual words more deeply is as important as knowing more words.

For children growing up in English-speaking families where adult–child talk is frequent and rich, rapid English vocabulary acquisition is the rule: According to Miller (1976, 1987), between the ages of 1 and 17, children add 13 words per day to their growing vocabulary, adding up to around 80,000 words by the time they are 17. Very little of this is achieved with the help of teachers or dictionaries. Vocabulary acquisition happens most easily in context and is related to topics that children care about. The teacher's responsibility lies mainly in setting up exposure to language in a vivid way and encouraging reading of engaging material at an appropriate level of complexity for the child.

For second language learners, new vocabulary items are best taught in related groups, so that words can be understood in connection with other words related to the same general topic. (For an accessible discussion of how the mental lexicon is thought to be organized, see Aitchison, 1994; for a discussion of how bilinguals and monolinguals differ in their treatment of words, see Merriman & Kutlesic, 1993.) Thus, talk about *mothers* and *fathers* should include talk about *brothers* and *sisters*, *grandfathers* and *grandmothers*; talk about *buying* should include talk about *selling*, *paying*, *money*, and *getting change*. Some understanding of how translations can differ from one another in subtle aspects of meaning and use can aid in supporting the lexical acquisition of the second language learner.

Are vernacular dialects different from "bad English" and if so, how?

Given the diversity of the social and cultural backgrounds of the students they serve, educational practitioners need a solid grounding in sociolinguistics and in language behavior across cultures. Like other languages, English has dialects associated with geographical regions and social classes and distinguished by contrasts in their sound system, grammar, and lexicon. Standard dialects are considered more prestigious than vernacular dialects, but this contrast is a matter of social convention alone. Vernacular dialects are as regular as standard dialects and as useful. Facts about normal language variation are not widely known, as demonstrated by the misunderstandings about language, language behavior, and language learning revealed in the national response to the Oakland (CA) School Board's 1996 Ebonics proposal. The proposal amounted to a declaration that the language spoken in the homes of many of its African American students should be regarded as a language in its own right, and should not be denigrated by teachers and administrators as slang, street talk, or bad English. It further declared the Board's support of the school district's efforts to seek funds for the Standard English Proficiency Program, which uses children's home language to teach school English. This idea was certainly not radical, but the Ebonics story continued to be news for nearly two months. It was the focus of talk shows on radio and television. It was featured in front-page newspaper stories for nearly a month, and even longer in editorial pages, political cartoons, and news magazines. The U.S. Senate held special hearings. The Oakland School Board's proposal was denounced, ripped apart, and ridiculed. Why was it controversial? This is how Delpit (1997) responded when asked, "What do you think about Ebonics? Are you for it or against it?"

My answer must be neither. I can be neither for Ebonics nor against Ebonics any more than I can be for or against air. It exists. It is the language spoken by many of our African-American children. It is the language they heard as their mothers nursed them and changed their diapers and played peek-a-boo with them. It is the language through which they first encountered love, nurturance, and joy. On the other hand, most teachers of those African-American children who have been least well-served by educational systems believe that their students' life chances will be further hampered if they do not learn Standard English. In the stratified society in which we live, they are absolutely correct. (Delpit, 1997: 6)

Schools must provide children who speak vernacular dialects of English the support they need to add a Standard English variety to broaden their skills for academic success and for jobs when they have completed school. The process is hindered when the language spoken by the children—the language of their families and primary communities—is disrespected in school. This is as true for a vernacular variety of English as it is for another language such as Navaho, Yup'ik, Cantonese, or Spanish. A recognition of how language figures in adults' perceptions of children is crucial to understanding what happens in schools and how children ultimately view schools and learning. How dialect differences affect language learning and literacy development depends in part on how vernacular dialect speakers are responded to at school. Practitioners need a good understanding about language variability in order to make educational decisions that ensure effective instruction and to prevent speakers of vernacular dialects from being misdiagnosed and misplaced in school programs. Knowledge of the natural course of language acquisition and of the capacity of the individual to maintain more than one dialect is crucial in making such choices. Knowledge about dialect differences can also enrich teaching about language in general, if dialects are treated respectfully and analytically in the classroom.

What is academic English?

Although there is a lot of discussion about the need for all children to develop the English language skills required for academic learning and development, few people can identify exactly what those skills consist of or distinguish them from general Standard English skills. In many cases, observers point to differences between written and spoken language, and they focus on vocabulary. In fact, academic English extends across both modalities, and it entails a broad range of language proficiencies that include, but go far beyond, knowledge of academic vocabulary. Understanding those proficiencies is now urgent, as the CCSS define "regular practice with academic language and complex texts" as required for upper elementary and secondary students (National Governors Association, 2010).

Uccelli and colleagues have recently developed an assessment of what they call Core Academic Language Skills (CALS) (see Uccelli & Phillips Galloway, this volume). CALS encompasses eight distinct, but correlated, domains of skill. One of the domains, for example, they call *information packing*—getting a lot of content into as few words as possible. Information packing can be accomplished through morphological modifications (e.g., a group from many nations → an international group; he invented the cotton gin → his invention) and through complex syntactic structures (e.g., the girl was tall. The girl loved cookies. The girl lived next door. → The tall girl who lived next door loved cookies.). The several dimensions of academic language define the skills that students need to understand the language of textbooks and assessments, to write effectively, and to engage in sophisticated classroom discussion.

A study of test items for a typical high school graduation examination reveals the centrality of academic language skills to success (Fillmore, 1999). To pass such tests, students have to be able to display the following capacities, all examples of specific domains identified by Uccelli and Phillips Galloway (this volume):

- Summarize texts, using linguistic cues to interpret and infer the writer's intentions and messages.
- Analyze texts, assessing the writer's use of language for rhetorical and aesthetic purposes, and to express perspective and mood.
- Extract meaning from texts and relate it to other ideas and information.
- Evaluate evidence and arguments presented in texts and critique the logic of their arguments.
- Recognize and analyze textual conventions used in various genres for special effect to trigger background knowledge or for perlocutionary effect.
- Recognize ungrammatical and infelicitous usage in written language and make necessary corrections to grammar, punctuation, and capitalization.
- Use grammatical devices for combining sentences into concise and more effective new ones, and use various devices to combine sentences into coherent and cohesive texts.
- Compose and write an extended, reasoned text that is well developed and supported with evidence and details.
- Interpret word problems—recognizing that in such texts, ordinary words may have specialized meanings (e.g., that *share equally among them* means to divide a whole into equal parts).
- Extract precise information from a written text and devise an appropriate strategy for solving the problem based on information provided in the text.

The production and understanding of academic English are issues for English learners and for native speakers of English alike. Few children arrive at school fully competent in the language required for text interpretation and for the kind of reasoned discourse we assume is a key to becoming an educated person. Possible exceptions are the children of academics and other highly educated professionals who use this register even at home, read a lot to their children, and engage them in discussions about a wide range of topics. For the most part, however, academic English is learned at school from teachers and from textbooks. Written texts are a reliable source of academic English, but they serve as the basis for language development only with instructional help. Teachers help students acquire this register when they go beyond discussions of content to discussions of the language used in texts for rhetorical and aesthetic effect. To provide such instructional support, teachers need to know something about how language figures in academic learning and to recognize that all students require instructional support and attention to acquire the forms and structures associated with it. This is especially true for English learners. Often, explicit teaching of language structures in the context of their use is the most effective way to help learners, as demonstrated by the classroom vignette in the prologue. Students are expected, according to the college- and career-ready standards, to engage in classroom discussions of sophisticated subject matter, using textual evidence to support well-formulated arguments. And teachers must know enough about academic language to predict where students will likely encounter challenges, and to decide what aspects should be explicitly taught and/or intensively practiced.

What kind of instructional support is needed for learning English?

Few students can develop oral and written English skills at the levels required for success in higher education or the workplace without well-designed instructional intervention, particularly if the only native English speakers they encounter in daily life are their teachers. In the 1970s and 1980s, teacher education programs relied heavily on research that emphasized the similarities between second and first language acquisition. This approach led to a belief that just being in an English-medium classroom was sufficient support for learning English, that no special instruction was needed. It is thus not surprising that teachers have been unclear about what instructional role they should play in second language learning.

Furthermore, these "natural" approaches do work to some degree and in some cases. But they ignore the sociolinguistic realities of many second language learners. These students need to be learning English very efficiently to meet the new, higher grade-level expectations. Evidence suggests that English learners acquire new vocabulary at the same rate as native English speakers (Mancilla-Martinez & Lesaux, 2011)—but of course they started later! They need to be learning faster than their English monolingual peers in order to catch up. That means that teachers need to provide explicit instruction in English vocabulary and grammar, rather than just using simplified English. Successful vocabulary interventions provide rich, recurrent exposures to new words, with planned opportunities for students to hear the words, spell the words, use the words in a variety of activities, and learn the concepts in which the words are embedded (e.g., Carlo *et al.*, 2004; Lesaux *et al.*, 2014; Proctor *et al.*, 2009).

Several decades ago, Fillmore (1982) pointed out that certain conditions must be met if young children are to be successful in second language learning. They must interact directly and frequently with people who know the language well enough to reveal how it works and how it can be used. During interactions with English learners, expert speakers not only provide access to the language at an appropriate level, but they also provide ample clues as to what the units in the language are and how they combine to communicate ideas, information, and intentions. Learners receive corrective feedback as they negotiate and clarify communicative intentions (Long, 1985; Pica, 1996). The acquisition process can go awry when the conditions for language learning are not met, especially when learners greatly outnumber people who know the language well enough to support acquisition, as in schools and classrooms with high populations of English learners. In such situations, instruction makes all the difference, but what matters most is the quality and focus of the instruction. Children require access to the kind of language they are supposed to be learning in order to learn it. For academic purposes, they need to learn the kind of language used in school—the language used in texts for school subjects like math and science, the language required for explanation and argumentation, the language of storybooks and poetry, too. Such language cannot be learned from others in the usual course of social interactions: It is learned from materials that use such language for academic purposes. This is where teachers play a crucial role. The teacher who was featured in the prologue to this chapter showed us how to make available to learners the relationship among meaning, communicative function, and language structures. By helping students look closely at a complex sentence from a text they were reading, she offered them a way to break into the code they were learning.

Without direct instruction in such situations, children may not develop their English skills as much as they could, or they might learn language forms from one another (Fillmore, 1991, 1992). In schools where English learners are segregated by proficiency level, or are expected to work on their own without instructional support from a teacher, progress is likely to be slow. In such situations, students may help one another, but since they are all second language learners, the outcome is likely to be "learnerese"—a fairly stable variety of English that learners speak fluently and confidently, but that does not meet the Standard English goal (these students are sometimes referred to as "ESL lifers" or "long-term English learners" because they remain in ESL classes for many years). In such cases, the assumption may be that these English learners just need to devote more time to studying English. However, devoting large amounts of school time to English instruction consisting of grammar, vocabulary, speaking, and writing exercises is unlikely to achieve second language success, especially when the study of language forms divorces them from the functions they serve—functions that are displayed in real reading, real writing, and content-area learning. Further, the students are left far behind in math, science, and social studies.

Better language outcomes for English learners can be facilitated if teachers know enough about the conditions for successful second language learning to scaffold students' access to rich English input. Educators must know enough about language learning and language itself to evaluate the appropriateness of various methods, materials, and approaches for helping students make progress in learning English—in particular when guidance from policymakers and educational leaders is weak.

Why has the acquisition of English by non-English-speaking children not been more universally successful?

It appears that non-English-speaking students may be having a harder and harder time learning English. Although it used to take from five to seven years to learn English to a high level (Cummins, 1981; Klesmer, 1994), recent studies suggest it is now taking longer than that for students to be reclassified as English proficient, perhaps due to instructional factors (Callahan, 2005; Conger et al., 2012) or perhaps to higher reclassification thresholds. Umansky and Reardon's (2014) analysis of 12 years of data on the reclassification of Latino English learners (to English proficient status) in a large California urban school district found that while English learners who have been in bilingual or dual language programs take somewhat longer to achieve the English proficiency level required for reclassification, they end up with academic and linguistic advantages over students who have been instructed in English-only programs. This study found that reclassification peaked at Grade 5, with a cumulative reclassification rate of 38%. Students who had not been reclassified at that point were designated by the state of California as "long-term English learners" (i.e., students classified as English learners longer than six years). In this district, 62% of all students who enter school as English learners become designated as long-term English learners. When they receive that label, their prospects for reclassification decline. Umansky and Reardon estimate the time to English proficiency in this district to be eight years, with a cumulative rate of reclassification of 50% at Grade 8; and 75% by Grade 11. Of all the students who began school as English learners, 25% were still classified as such at the end of high school. This issue is not limited to the school district in which the research was conducted, or to California schools, or to Latino students (Conger *et al.*, 2012; Menken, 2013). The problem affects many students. Both background factors (Greenberg Motamedi *et al.*, 2016; Thompson, 2015) and instructional factors (Callahan, 2005; Menken, 2013; Olsen, 2010) have been implicated. Students who are not reclassified in a timely fashion come to be seen as problematic and tend to be streamed into classes where the emphasis is on remediation of basic skills. Students who are designated as English learners in high school tend to be tracked into classes offering limited opportunities for academic advancement (Callahan, 2005; Kanno & Kangas, 2014).

Written language

Written language is not merely oral language written down. To help their students acquire literacy, teachers need to know how written language contrasts with speech. Here we discuss questions about written language that teachers should be able to answer.

Why is English spelling so complicated?

Since the first sound in *sure* and *sugar* is different from the first sound in *sun* or *super*, why aren't these words spelled differently? Why don't we spell the /s/ sound in *electricity* with an *s*? Why are there so many peculiar spellings among highly frequent words like *have*, *said*, *might*, and *could*? How can *oo* spell three different vowel sounds, as we discover when we hear vampires and mosquitoes say to one another before dining: "Blood is good food!"?

These and other peculiarities of English spelling reflect two facts about English orthography:

- Unlike French, Spanish, Dutch, and many other languages, English has never had a language academy charged with regular review and reform of spelling to eliminate inconsistencies and reflect language change.
- English generally retains the spelling of morphological units, even when the rules of pronunciation mean that phonemes within these morphological units vary (e.g., *electric*, *electricity*, *electrician*).

These two forces have led to what is called a *deep orthography* for English—an orthography in which the match of sound and spelling is complex and dependent on many factors. This is not to say that English spelling is illogical, irrational, or impossible to teach. However, some insight into the forces that have generated English spelling patterns can help teachers teach more effectively and understand children's errors.

It is helpful to consider the wide array of writing systems that exist in the world's languages (see Daniels & Bright, 1996). Some languages, such as Chinese, represent morphemes—semantically meaningful units—with their graphemic symbols (characters). Others, such as the Japanese katakana system, represent syllables instead. Both of these systems (morphemic and syllabic) have the advantage of being rather easy for young children, since morphemes and syllables are more psychologically accessible than phonemes, which are more abstract than syllabic or morphemic units and often difficult to segment or pronounce in isolation. In alphabetic writing systems, letters (technically, graphemes) typically represent phonemes. Representing sounds alphabetically is fairly straightforward in languages that have experienced spelling reform, such as Spanish, and those that have adopted writing rather recently, such as Hmong. English, though, like Danish and German to some extent, often ignores phoneme identity to preserve the spelling identity of morphemes. For example, in English the spelling *s* is used for plural morphemes whether they are pronounced [s] or [z]—even though in other contexts, such as at the beginning of words, the [s] and [z] sounds are spelled distinctively. Compare the spelling and pronunciation of the ending of *dogs* and *cats* to the first sound in *zoo* and in *Sue*. Similarly, the root form *electric* is retained even in forms where the final *c* represents quite a different sound from the [k] in *electric*, including the [s] of *electricity* and the [š] of *electrician*.

The fact that the spelling *electric* is retained in all related word forms actually makes reading and inferring word meanings easier. Similarly, there is an advantage to writing *t* in both *complete* and *completion*, or in both *activity* and *action*, even though the sounds that it stands for vary. The spelling makes it easier to see that the two words are morphologically related. For the same reason, it is probably good that we use the same letter for the three different vowel sounds that occur between *p* and *t* in the words *compete*, *competitive*, and *competition*. Those advantages to accessing word meaning while reading, though, come at some cost to the ease of initial reading instruction.

Other aspects of English spelling are less helpful. For example, the *gh* in words like *night*, *through*, and *thought* is left over from a sound that has long since disappeared from English. Such spellings signal etymological relationships with words in other Germanic languages. English also tends to retain spellings that indicate the source of borrowed words, such as *ph* for /f/ and *y* for /ai/ in Greek origin words (*phone*, *hypothesis*). Such patterns increase the etymological information available to the reader, but they do exacerbate the problems of decoding and spelling.

Some understanding of such complexities in English orthography can help teachers take sensible approaches to teaching the alphabetic principle in English. When teachers know about the sound system of English and the history of language contact and development that has affected our writing system, they will better understand why simplistic phonics approaches are inadvisable in teaching English reading.

Errors in spelling English can result from writers' inclination to write what they hear. Second language speakers' spelling errors can reflect inadequate exposure to written English forms, lack of adequate instruction in the nature of the English orthographic system, or transfer of general spelling strategies from another language. Some languages with alphabetic systems, such as Arabic or Tigrinya, are basically syllabic in their written representation: They focus on spelling the consonants in syllables, designating the vowels sketchily or omitting them entirely. Some languages, such as Spanish, with spelling systems that are quite phonemic, adjust spellings to reflect pronunciation even in closely related words (compare, for example, the related forms *saco* and *saque*). Some other languages resemble English in representing historical facts in their spelling, retaining information about the source language of borrowed lexical items (e.g., Persian and Japanese). Knowing how the orthographies of different languages are organized can help teachers figure out what sorts of spelling rules learners are likely to find easy or hard, what first language skills learners can rely on, and why students make certain types of errors. Understanding that there can be substantial differences in how symbols are used to represent sounds in different languages will help teachers be more effective in working with students who have had some prior literacy instruction in their native languages—students who have learned to read in Spanish, Vietnamese, French, and so forth before entering an English reading program. The relationship between sounds and symbols can be relatively simple and straightforward in one language and much more complex in another.

Why do some children have more trouble than others in developing early reading skills?

The problems beginning readers encounter can seem overwhelming and incomprehensible to a teacher who has not had a chance to learn about the complexities of the reading process. Knowledge about language is crucial in helping teachers do a better job of teaching initial reading (Snow *et al.*, 1998). Effective reading instruction requires integrating attention to the system of phoneme/grapheme mappings with attention to meaning. Children may encounter difficulties because they do not understand the basic principle of alphabetic writing—that letters represent sounds—or because they cannot segment the sounds reliably, or because they don't know the words they are expected to be reading. Second language learners are particularly likely to find difficulties in producing, remembering, and distinguishing the target phonemes and to lack the knowledge of how words are pronounced that would help them in decoding (Ruddell & Unrau, 1997).

An additional problem arises when teachers give tutors or teacher aides the responsibility for teaching reading to children who need the most help. These individuals are far less qualified to teach reading than are teachers. Even more problematic, teachers may assign English learners to peer tutors for help with reading on the grounds that children can communicate more effectively with other children than adults can. It takes a solid understanding of language to teach reading effectively, especially to children who are having the greatest difficulty grasping the abstract and complex relationships between sound and print, and who may be unfamiliar with the ideas that the print is trying to convey. Teachers cannot make learning to read in English effortless, but they should be clearly aware of where and why the difficulties exist.

What makes a sentence or a text easy or difficult to understand?

Many educators associate simple, short sentences with ease in understanding and interpretation. For that reason, texts that are prepared and selected for English learners and other struggling readers are often composed of short, choppy sentences. The result is unnatural, incoherent text conveying less substance than regular texts. One teacher described the materials being used with fourth-grade ESL students as "first grade materials, very basic—it isn't *see Spot run*, but it's close" (Gebhard, 2000). Do greatly simplified materials help or hurt comprehension? An examination of texts that had been modified according to the readability formulas used by textbook publishers found that such texts are often more difficult to interpret (Davison & Kantor, 1982). These texts require the reader to infer how sentences relate to each other, because to make sentences short, words and grammatical structures that show rhetorical or narrative connections between ideas—precisely the features identified above as academic language—are often eliminated.

The following text exemplifies the modifications found in simplified textbooks for low-achieving and ESL students:

Using limestone to make other things

We can use limestone to make other useful materials. To do this we have to use chemical reactions.

Limestone is a rock that is made mostly from calcium carbonate.

If you heat limestone strongly you produce a gas called carbon dioxide. The substance left behind is called calcium oxide.

Calcium oxide is also called quicklime. (Milner *et al.*, 1998: 174)

Text simplification is achieved by restricting the number of words used. This text contains just 61 words, distributed among 7 sentences, including the heading. The average number of words per sentence for this text is 8.7. Tight constraints on length become a greater concern than any other criteria that might guide the preparation of such a text, such as informativeness, relevance, coherence, naturalness, and grace. The end result is that such texts are not only uninspiring and insulting to the reader, but often harder to comprehend than the normal texts for that grade level (Graesser *et al.*, 2003).

Because simplified texts are often unnatural, they cannot serve as exemplars of written academic English. Well-written texts with grade-level-appropriate language can give students access to the register of English that is used in academic writing (Fillmore & Fillmore, 2012). With the help of teachers as knowledgeable as the one who conducted the "wires-behind-the-walls" lesson presented above, students can use these texts to learn the vocabulary, grammatical structures, phraseology, and rhetorical devices associated with that register. Exposure to such sentences provides both more information and a better model of language use. Even low-proficiency speakers of English can understand long and complex sentences—"juicy sentences"—given the right support (Fillmore, 2014). Learning to understand and produce academic English is a goal not only for English learners but for native speakers of English too.

Teachers and school administrators play a nontrivial role in determining how textbooks are written. Because textbook publishers can stay in business only if states and school districts adopt their materials, they tend to be attuned to what educators want. In the process of designing curricula, publishers produce prototype materials that they market test on school administrators who they hope will purchase the texts and on teachers who they hope will select them. Educators need to develop a sure sense about what is appropriate for students at different grade levels so that they can make wise decisions in selecting and using text materials. To do that, they need to know enough about language to assess the appropriateness of the language used in texts, particularly for students who are learning English or who are having difficulty learning to read.

Why do students have trouble with structuring narrative and expository writing?

All students need to learn the rhetorical structures associated with storytelling, exposition, and argumentation in English. However, some students bring to this task culturally based text structures that contrast with those expected at schools. The emphasis in mainstream English stories is on getting the order of events correct and clear. This emphasis can seem so obviously right to a monolingual speaker of English that the narrative of the Latino child, which emphasizes personal relationships more than plot, or of the Japanese child, who may provide very terse stories rather than recounting all of the events, may be dismissed as incomprehensible (McCabe, 1995). Different cultures focus on different aspects of an episode. Evaluating a child's story requires understanding what aspects of the narrative the child considers important. Guiding students in acquiring the story structures valued at school is more effective if teachers understand how the school structure differs from the first language preferences.

Expository and argument structures also vary considerably across cultures. There is no best way to make a point: Different ways make sense in different cultures. The topic sentences, paragraphs, and compare-and-contrast essays that are staples of English prose may be quite opaque for students whose language experience includes other structures. Understanding that some of these features may be absent or very differently structured in literacy traditions associated with other languages can be very helpful for teachers. In particular, it may prevent them from mistakenly attributing language or cognitive disorders to students who have simply transferred a native language rhetorical style to English.

What other issues need to be considered for student writing development?

Educators must have a solid enough knowledge of grammatical concepts, as well as an understanding of the special features of academic language, to support children's writing development. They need to make use of information about grammatical structure to pinpoint the problems many students have in writing or interpreting text, and they need to be able to teach students about language structures that they can draw on in their writing. Partly because teachers feel insecure about their own knowledge of grammar, and partly because teachers of writing are sometimes reluctant to correct students' writing, students may not get the kind of informative feedback they need in order to become more effective writers. The problem is particularly acute for learners of ESL.

The consequences of not addressing writing development issues adequately may not surface until after high school, when many first-year college students—English learners and native English speakers alike—discover that the English and literacy skills they bring with them do not enable them to handle college-level literacy demands. A study by the National Center for Public Policy and Higher Education (2010: 1) found that across the nation, "nearly 60% of first-year college students discover that, despite being fully eligible to attend college, they are not academically ready for postsecondary studies."

Helping students who are struggling with academic discourse calls for professional development for teachers, such as that devised by Robin Scarcella, a specialist in language and literacy development and director of the Academic English Program at the University of California at Irvine. For many years, the program was focused on teaching ESL. It served many academically talented and highly qualified former English learners who, despite high SAT scores and stellar grade point averages from high school, lacked the language or literacy skills required for university-level coursework. Their English writing indicated that they did not have a sure sense of how English works. Over the years, the program has expanded to give broader support and it now serves as a model for the other nine campuses of the University of California, where 79% of the entering students had to take the academic writing placement test in 2013. Of those who did, the 59% who failed needed to take coursework to prepare them for the writing demands of college courses. To support teachers who work with students needing this assistance, Scarcella (2003) prepared an open-source professional development handbook for the University of California focused on language and literacy development that offers suggestions for ensuring that students are ready for college when they graduate from high school.

How can teachers better prepare students for university expectations in literacy? Assigning more writing tasks, providing engaging topics to motivate investment in writing, providing lots of texts that offer grist for written arguments and explanations, and giving feedback on the correctness and appropriateness of the students' writing would certainly help. Making feedback appropriate and useful requires a deep understanding of the characteristics of English grammar and of academic language, as well as of good argument structure.

Target Domains for Teacher Learning

Although it would go beyond our brief to propose any specific curriculum for teacher education, we offer here some suggestions for topics that should be covered in preservice and/or in-service learning for teachers. These address fundamental issues in the education of English learners and other students for whom literacy and language learning in school contexts might be problematic.

Language and linguistics

An introductory understanding of linguistics motivated by the educational considerations we have mentioned—language structure, language in literacy development, language use in educational settings, the history of English, and the basics of linguistic analysis—would be of great value. We envision linking every topic to educational situations in which language is an issue. For example, learning about phonology could begin with an examination of interference problems that English learners might have with the English sound system. It might include investigation of topics such as why speakers of Cantonese or Spanish have problems with consonant clusters at the ends of English words like *sixths*, which contains four consonants in a row at the end /sɪksəs/. Similarly, learning about argument structure could start with a discourse analysis of what makes for a highly valued, "A+" argument in Chinese, in Spanish, and in English.

Language and cultural diversity

Cultural contrasts in language use that are likely to surface in teaching and learning could easily be exemplified by attention to cultural/linguistic differences in conversational rules (how long do you wait to be sure the person speaking is finished?), in address forms (which adults are spoken to with first names, with pseudo-kin terms like "auntie," with Mr. or Ms.?), in proxemics (how close do you stand to other people? Who can you look in the face?), in speaking rights (who gets to say "I don't understand" or "I can't hear you"? How should one respond to questions with obvious answers?), in narrative forms (what events are worth telling about? Is plot or character or evaluation most important?), and so on.

Sociolinguistics for educators in a linguistically diverse society

Educators need to understand the social and sociolinguistic forces behind the language policies and politics that affect schools, including language attitudes in intergroup relations that affect students and language values. Language contact, language shift and loss or isolation, the role and the history of bilingualism in schools and society, and fundamental understandings about the nature of dialects and their connection to social identity are all crucial topics for educators to understand.

Language development

Educators need to understand the process of language development, with a special focus on academic language development in school-aged children—native speakers of both vernacular and Standard English dialects, as well as those who speak other languages. The role of literacy in the development of language skills and the acquisition of the structures and vocabulary required for further literacy development also need attention.

Second language learning and teaching

Theoretical and practical knowledge about how second language acquisition proceeds and the factors that affect it is crucial for educators. It is instructive to compare second language learning to first language learning and to examine the role of the primary language in second language learning. Educators need access to research specifying just how orally proficient children must be in a second language before they can learn to read and write in that language.

The language of academic discourse

Many educators are unaware of how different academic English is from the language of informal communication. The language structures specific to different domains of content learning—science, social science, math, and so on—have been explored and to some extent specified (Shanahan & Shanahan, 2008). Teachers who are experts in those content areas may well be fluent in the language of their disciplines without realizing how distinct it is from the language their students use.

Text analysis and language understanding in educational settings

Educators need to understand how language structures and style in written texts affect comprehensibility, not just in order to choose texts, but also to decide where to put extra instructional attention within texts. The needs of English learners and vernacular dialect speakers in processing and producing text deserve special attention.

Conclusion

We have sketched here the reasons that educators need to know about language, the kinds of knowledge about language that they need, and an inventory of topics that would cover this crucial core of knowledge in teacher learning. This proposal may strike some readers as utopian. We acknowledge that we have formulated it without thinking about the structures and constraints of traditional teacher education or in-service programs. Nonetheless, we are energized by the current educational policy environment, marked by continuing debates about educating English learners, growing awareness of the challenges of disciplinary literacy, rising efforts to meet internationally benchmarked literacy standards, and urgent searches for better literacy instruction, especially in the post-primary grades. The substance of the discussion around these issues gives striking testimony to the historical paucity of relevant expertise on language among those who are in the best position to improve public knowledge—educational practitioners (see, for example, Goldman & Snow, 2015; RAND, 2002; Snow *et al.*, 1998).

It is clear that many of the challenges we face in education stem from the fact that ours is a diverse society. Students in our schools come from virtually every corner of the planet, and they bring to school diverse outlooks, languages, cultural beliefs and behaviors, and background experiences. Teachers in our schools have not always known what to do with the differences they encounter in their classrooms. As a society, we expect them to educate whoever shows up at the schoolhouse, to provide their students with the language and literacy skills to survive in school and later on in jobs, to teach them all of the school subjects that they will need to know about as adults, and to prepare them in other ways for higher education and for the workplace. What does it take for teachers to handle this challenge? We must be clear about how daunting a task this is, and how much support many teachers will need if they are to work effectively with all their students. We have argued that basic coursework in educational linguistics is one key element in preparing teachers for today's schools.

Acknowledgments

The authors are grateful to the many educators who have shared their insights on language with us. They especially thank Chris Anderle, the science teacher featured in the prologue, who showed us what a difference a teacher who knows how language works in teaching and learning can make in the academic development of her students. They also thank colleagues who contributed comments on an earlier version of this chapter and supplied examples: Eve Agee, Kathleen Brown, Maria Carlo, Charles J. Fillmore, Peg Griffin, Marita Hopmann, Joy Kreeft Peyton, and Nicolas Zavala.

References

Aitchison, J. (1994) *Words in the Mind: An Introduction to the Mental Lexicon.* Oxford: Blackwell.

Artiles, A.J., Rueda, R., Salazar, J.J. and Higareda, I. (2005) Within-group diversity in minority disproportionate representation: English learners in urban school districts. *Exceptional Children* 71, 283–300.

August, D. and Shanahan, T. (2006) *Developing Literacy in Second-Language Learners: Report of the National Literacy Panel on Language Minority Children and Youth.* Mahwah, NJ: Lawrence Erlbaum.

Avineri, N., Blum, S., Johnson, E., Riley, K. and Zentella, A. (2016) The gap that won't be filled: An anthropolitical critique of the 'language gap'. *Anthropology News*, Society for Linguistic Anthropology, August 2016. Available for purchase at http://onlinelibrary.wiley.com/doi/10.1111/AN.111/pdf.

Beck, I.L., McKeown, M.G. and Kucan, L. (2002) *Bringing Words to Life: Robust Vocabulary Instruction.* New York: The Guilford Press.

Bereiter, C. and Englemann, S. (1966) *Teaching Disadvantaged Children in the Preschool.* Englewood Cliffs, NJ: Prentice-Hall.

Berman, R. (2004) Between emergence and mastery: The long developmental route of language acquisition. In R. Berman (ed.) *Language Development across Childhood and Adolescence* (pp. 9–34). Philadelphia, PA: John Benjamins Publishing Co.

Bernstein, B. (1971) *Class, Codes and Control* (Vol. 1). London: Routledge & Kegan Paul.

Callahan, R. (2005) Tracking and high school English learners: Limiting opportunity to learn. *American Educational Research Journal* 42 (2), 305–328.

Carlo, M., August, D., McLaughlin, B., Snow, C., Dressler, C., Lippman, D., Lively, T. and White, C. (2004) Closing the gap: Addressing the vocabulary needs of English learners in bilingual and mainstream classrooms. *Reading Research Quarterly* 39 (2), 188–215.

Conger, D., Hatch, M., McKinney, J., Atwell, M.S. and Lamb, A. (2012) *Time to English Proficiency for English Learners in New York City and Miami-Dade County.* New York: The Institute for Educational and Social Policy.

Cummins, J. (1981) Age on arrival and immigrant second language learning in Canada: A reassessment. *Applied Linguistics* 2, 132–149.

Daniels, P. and Bright, W. (1996) *The World's Writing Systems.* New York: Oxford University Press.

Davison, A. and Kantor, R. (1982) On the failure of readability formulas to define readable texts: A case study from adaptations. *Reading Research Quarterly* 17 (2), 187–209.

Delpit, L. (1997) Ebonics and culturally responsive instruction. *Rethinking Schools (Special Ebonics Issue)* 12 (1), 1–7.

Duncan, G.J. and Murnane, R.J. (2014) *Restoring Opportunity: The Crisis of Inequality and the Challenge for American Education.* Cambridge, MA: Harvard Education Press and the Russell Sage Foundation.

Fillmore, L.W. (1982) Instructional language as linguistic input: Second language learning in classrooms. In L.C. Wilkinson (ed.) *Communicating in the Classroom* (pp. 283–296). New York: Academic Press.

Fillmore, L.W. (1991) Second-language learning in children: A model of language learning in social context. In E. Bialystok (ed.) *Language Processing in Bilingual Children* (pp. 49–69). New York: Cambridge University Press.

Fillmore, L.W. (1992) Learning a language from learners. In C. Kramsch and S. McConnell-Ginet (eds) *Text and Context: Cross-Disciplinary Perspectives on Language Study* (pp. 46–66). Lexington, MA: D.C. Heath.

Fillmore, L.W. (1999, February) The class of 2002: Will everyone be there? Paper presented at the Alaska State Department of Education, Anchorage, AK.

Fillmore, L.W. (2014) English learners at the crossroads of educational reform. *TESOL Quarterly* 48 (3), 624–632. doi: 10.1002/tesq.174.

Fillmore, L.W. and Fillmore, C. (2012) What does text complexity mean for English learners and language minority students? Paper presented at the Understanding Language Conference, Stanford, CA. See http://ell.stanford.edu/publication/what-does-text-complexity-mean-english-learners-and-language-minority-students (accessed 2 March 2018).

Fuller, B. and García Coll, C. (2010) Learning from Latinos: Contexts, families, and child development in motion. *Developmental Psychology* 46 (3), 559–565.

Gebhard, M.L. (2000) Reconceptualizing classroom second language acquisition as an instructional phenomenon. Unpublished doctoral dissertation, University of California at Berkeley.

Goldman, S. and Snow, C.E. (2015) Adolescent literacy: Development and instruction. In A. Pollatsek and R. Treiman (eds) *Handbook on Reading* (pp. 463–478). Oxford: Oxford University Press.

Graesser, A.C., McNamara, D.S. and Louwerse, M.M. (2003) What do readers need to learn in order to process coherence relations in narrative and expository text? In A.P. Sweet and C.E. Snow (eds) *Rethinking Reading Comprehension* (pp. 82–98). New York: Guilford Publications Press.

Greenberg Motamedi, J., Singh, M. and Thompson, K. (2016) *English Student Characteristics and Time to Reclassification: An Example from Washington State.* (REL 2016-128). Washington, DC: U.S. Department of Education, Institute of Education Sciences, National Center for Educational Evaluation and Regional Assistance, Regional Educational Laboratory Northwest. See http://ies.ed.gov/ncee/edlabs/ (accessed 2 March 2018).

Hart, B. and Risley, T.R. (1995) *Meaningful Differences in the Everyday Experiences of Young American Children.* Baltimore, MD: Brookes.

Hart, B. and Risley, T.R. (2003) The early catastrophe: The 30 million word gap by age 3. *American Educator* 27 (1), 4–9. See http://www.aft.org/sites/default/files/periodicals/TheEarlyCatastrophe.pdf (accessed 2 March 2018).

Heath, S.B. (1983) *Ways with Words: Language, Life, and Work in Communities and Classrooms.* New York: Cambridge University Press.

Hehir, T. and Mosqueda, E. (2007) San Diego Unified School District Special Education Issues Document, Final Report, submitted to the San Diego Unified School District. See https://www.sandiegounified.org/sites/default/files_link/district/files/special-education/relatedfiles/HehirReport/hehir_issues.pdf (accessed 2 March 2018).

Hoyle, S. and Adger, C.T. (1998) Introduction. In S.M. Hoyle and C.T. Adger (eds) *Kids Talk: Strategic Language Use in Later Childhood* (pp. 3–22). New York: Oxford University Press.

Kanno, Y. and Kangas, S. (2014) "I'm not going to be, like, for the AP": English learners' limited access to advanced college-preparatory courses in high school. *American Educational Research Journal* 51 (5), 848–878.

Kent, L. (2015) 5 facts about America's students. *Fact Tank: News in the Numbers.* Pew Research Center, August 10, 2015. See http://www.pewresearch.org/fact-tank/2015/08/10/5-facts-about-americas-students/ (accessed 2 March 2018).

Klesmer, H. (1994) Assessment and teacher perceptions of ESL student achievement. *English Quarterly* 26 (3), 8–11.

Lesaux, N.K., Kieffer, M.J., Kelley, J.G. and Harris, J.R. (2014) Effects of academic vocabulary instruction for linguistically diverse adolescents: Evidence from a randomized field trial. *American Educational Research Journal* 51 (6), 1159–1194.

Linn, D. and Hemmer, L. (2011) English learner disproportionality in special education: Implications for the scholar-practitioner. *Journal of Educational Research and Practice* 1 (1), 70–80.

Lleras, C. and Rangel, C. (2009) Ability grouping practices in elementary school and African American/Hispanic achievement. *American Journal of Education* 115 (2), 279–304.

Long, M.H. (1985) Input and second language acquisition theory. In S.M. Gass and C.G. Madden (eds) *Input in Second Language Acquisition* (pp. 377–393). Rowley, MA: Newbury House.

Loveless, T. (2013) The resurgence of ability grouping and persistence of tracking. *The 2013 Brown Center Report on American Education, Part II* (pp. 12–21). Washington, DC: The Brookings Institution.

Mancilla-Martinez, J. and Lesaux, N.K. (2011) The gap between Spanish-speakers' word reading and word knowledge: A longitudinal study. *Child Development* 82, 1544–1560.

McCabe, A. (1995) *Chameleon Readers: Teaching Children to Appreciate All Kinds of Good Stories.* New York: McGraw-Hill.

Meier, T. (2008) *Black Communications and Learning to Read: Building on Children's Linguistic and Cultural Strengths.* New York: Lawrence Erlbaum Associates.

Menken, K. (2013) Emergent bilingual students in secondary school: Along the academic language and literacy continuum. *Language Teaching* 46 (4), 438–476.

Menyuk, P. and Brisk, M.E. (2005) *Language Development and Education: Children with Varying Language Experiences.* London: Palgrave Macmillan.

Merriman, W.E. and Kutlesic, V. (1993) Bilingual and monolingual children's use of two lexical acquisition heuristics. *Applied Linguistics* 14, 229–249.

Michaels, S. (2013) Déjà vu all over again: What's wrong with Hart & Risley and a 'linguistic deficit' framework in early childhood education? *Learning Landscapes* 7 (1), 23–41.

Miller, G.A. (1976) *Spontaneous Apprentices: Children and Language.* New York: Seabury Press.

Miller, G.A. (1987) How children learn words. In F. Marshall (ed.) *Proceedings of the Third Eastern Conference on Linguistics* (pp. 73–89). Columbus, OH: The Ohio State University.

Miller, P.J. and Sperry, D.E. (2012) Déjà vu: The continuing misrecognition of low-income children's verbal abilities. In S.T. Fiske and H.R. Markus (eds) *Facing Social Class: How Societal Rank Influences Interaction* (pp. 109–130). New York: Russell Sage.

Milner, B., Martin, J. and Evans, P. (1998) *Core Science* (Key Concepts). Cambridge: Cambridge University Press.

Moreno, R. and Pérez-Granados, D. (2002) Understanding language socialization and learning in Mexican-descent families: Conclusions and new directions. *Hispanic Journal of Behavioral Sciences* 24, 249–256.

Murnane, R.J. and Levy, F. (1996) *Teaching the New Basic Skills: Principles for Educating Children to Thrive in a Changing Economy*. New York: Free Press.

National Academies of Sciences, Engineering, and Medicine (2017) *Promoting the Educational Success of Children and Youth Learning English: Promising Futures*. Washington, DC: The National Academies Press. doi: 10.17226/24677.

National Center for Public Policy and Higher Education, and the Southern Regional Education Board (2010) Beyond the Rhetoric: Improving College Readiness through Coherent State Policy. See http://www.highereducation.org/reports/college_readiness/CollegeReadiness.pdf (accessed 2 March 2018).

National Governors Association Center for Best Practices and Council of Chief State School Officers (2010) Appendix A: Research supporting key elements of the standards. In *Common Core State Standards for English Language Arts & Literacy in History/Social Studies, Science and Technical Subjects*. Washington, DC: National Governors Association Center for Best Practices and Council of Chief State School Officers.

Oakes, J. (1985) *Keeping Track: How Schools Structure Inequality*. New Haven, CT: Yale University Press.

Olsen, L. (2010) *Reparable Harm: Fulfilling the Unkept Promise of Educational Opportunity for California's Long Term English Learners*. Long Beach, CA: Californians Together.

Philips, S.U. (1993) *The Invisible Culture: Communication in the Classroom and Community on the Warm Springs Indian Reservation* (2nd edn). New York: Free Press.

Pica, T. (1996) Second language learning through interaction: Multiple perspectives. *Working Papers in Educational Linguistics* 12, 1–22.

Pinker, S. (1999) *Words and Rules: The Ingredients of Language*. New York: Perseus Books.

Popovi Da (1969) Indian values. *Southwest Association of Indian Affairs Quarterly* 6, 15–19.

Proctor, C.P., Uccelli, P., Dalton, B. and Snow, C.E. (2009) Understanding depth of vocabulary online with bilingual and monolingual children. *Reading and Writing Quarterly* 22, 311–333.

RAND Reading Study Group (C. Snow, Chair) (2002) *Reading for Understanding: Toward an R&D Program in Reading Comprehension*. Santa Monica, CA: RAND Corporation.

Reyes, I. and Moll, L.C. (2008) Bilingual and biliterate practices at home and school. In B. Spolsky and F.M. Hult (eds) *The Handbook of Educational Linguistics* (pp. 147–160). Malden, MA: Blackwell Publishing.

Rodriguez, R. (1982) *Hunger of Memory: The Autobiography of Richard Rodriguez*. Toronto/New York: Bantam Books.

Romero-Little, M.E. (2004) Cultural literacy in the world of pueblo children. In E. Gregory, S. Long and D. Volk (eds) *Many Pathways to Literacy: Young Children Learning with Siblings, Grandparents, Peers and Communities* (pp. 208–220). New York: Routledge-Falmer.

Ruddell, R.B. and Unrau, N.J. (1997) The role of responsive teaching in focusing reader attention and developing reader motivation. In J.T. Guthrie and A. Wigfield (eds) *Reading Engagement: Motivating Readers through Integrated Instruction* (pp. 102–125). Newark, DE: International Reading Association.

Ruiz Soto, A., Hooker, S. and Batalova, J. (2015) *Top Languages Spoken by English Learners Nationally and by State*. Washington, DC: Migration Policy Institute.

Scarcella, R. (2003) Academic English: A Conceptual Framework. Technical Report 2003-1. Santa Barbara, CA: The University of California Linguistic Minority Research Institute.

Schecter, S.R. and Bayley, R. (2002) *Language as Cultural Practice: Mexicanos en el Norte*. Mahwah, NJ: Lawrence Erlbaum.

Shanahan, T. and Shanahan, C. (2008) Teaching disciplinary literacy to adolescents. *Harvard Educational Review* 78, 40–59.

Smitherman, G. (1977) *Talkin and testifyin: The Language of Black America*. Detroit, MI: Wayne State University Press.

Snow, C. (2017) The role of vocabulary versus knowledge in children's language learning: A fifty-year perspective. *Infancia y Aprendizaje: Journal for the Study of Education and Development* 40 (1), 1–18.

Snow, C.E., Burns, M.S. and Griffin, P. (eds) (1998) *Preventing Reading Difficulties in Young Children*. Washington, DC: National Academy Press.

Sullivan, A.L. (2011) Disproportionality in special education identification and placement of English learners. *Exceptional Children* 77 (3), 317–334.

Tharp, R.G., Jordan, C., Speidel, G., Au, K.H-P., Klein, T.W., Calkins, R.P., Sloat, K.C.M. and Gallimore, R. (2007) Education and Native Hawaiian children: Revisiting KEEP. *Hülili: Multidisciplinary Research on Hawaiian Well-Being* 4 (1), 269–317.

Thompson, K.D. (2015) English learners' time to reclassification: An analysis. *Educational Policy* 31 (3), 330–363.

Tolchinsky, L. (2004) The nature and scope of later language development. In R. Berman (ed.) *Language Development across Childhood and Adolescence* (pp. 233–248). Philadelphia, PA: John Benjamins Publishing Co.

Umansky, I.M. and Reardon, S.F. (2014) Reclassification patterns among Latino English learner students in bilingual, dual immersion, and English immersion classrooms. *American Educational Research Journal* 51 (5), 879–912.

Valdés, G. (1996) *Con Respeto: Bridging the Distances between Culturally Diverse Families and Schools: An Ethnographic Portrait*. New York: Teachers College Press.

Wong, J.S. (1989) *Fifth Chinese Daughter*. Seattle, WA: University of Washington Press. (Original work published, 1945.)

Wyman, L. (2012) *Youth Culture, Language Endangerment and Linguistic Survivance*. Bristol: Multilingual Matters.

Zentella, A.C. (1997) *Growing Up Bilingual*. Malden, MA: Blackwell.

2 Analyzing *Themes*: Knowledge About Language for Exploring Text Structure

Mary J. Schleppegrell

As Fillmore and Snow (this volume, p. 13) point out, the Common Core State Standards "shift the emphasis in literacy instruction radically—away from words toward text, from accuracy toward interpretation, evaluation, and synthesis, and from summarization toward argumentation." While they see this as a positive move, they point out that teaching students to succeed at these challenging tasks requires knowledge about language and how it works. Teachers need to know that texts are shaped by the language choices of their authors as they craft texts for different purposes and that exploring the ways that texts unfold can help students read with greater comprehension. In teacher education courses, participants often learn about text organization patterns such as sequence, description, cause and effect, comparison/contrast, or problem/solution, but these patterns seldom show up neatly in the authentic texts that students read. The advice given to recognize text structure seldom goes beyond a focus on very explicit connecting phrases (*first, finally* as markers of sequence) or conjunctions (*because, if* as signals of cause or condition) that are not always present in the texts that students read. This chapter introduces knowledge about language that can help teachers explore text structure with their students by analyzing how the words and phrases that begin a sentence shape and direct the unfolding of texts of different genres.

Texts are not arbitrary collections of sentences. Instead, each sentence in a text builds from what has come before and moves toward what will come next. Linguists who take a functional perspective on language have shown how sentence beginnings shape texts in ways that teachers can talk about with students to help them understand meaning and recognize how different genres are structured. Drawing on Halliday's systemic functional linguistics (SFL), they have used its functional grammar to engage students in meaningful talk about language in school texts (Derewianka, 2011; Fang & Schleppegrell, 2008).

Halliday (1980/2004) points out that children encounter language in the classroom in three ways: They are always learning language, learning through language, and learning about language, but learning about language is sometimes neglected or not made meaningful, as Fillmore and Snow (this volume) observe. By linking language forms with the meanings they present, Halliday's (1994) SFL offers a functional grammar that provides new ways for teachers to support the learning about language that will help students continue to learn through language. SFL offers new ways of talking with students about the language in the texts they read and about the language choices they can make in their own writing.

Analyzing Sentence Themes to Recognize Text Structure

Theme is a construct of functional grammar that can be identified to recognize how a text is organized and how its meanings evolve across the text as a whole. The Theme is the first grammatical constituent in the clause, so it can be readily identified even by those new to thinking and talking about language structure. Let's look at an example (Themes in italics):

> *Sara and Kylie* were best friends. *At school*, they ate lunch together and played together during recess every day. *They* had play dates every Saturday afternoon. *But during the summer*, Kylie's family went to Maine, and Sara's family stayed in Michigan.
>
> *For the first couple of weeks apart*, they would send emails to one another. *They* both wished summer would end quickly. *But the emailing* eventually stopped. *Kylie* started enjoying her time at the beach, and Sara forgot to write emails because she spent hours reading and drawing in her tree house. (From "Best Friends" by Carrie Symons, unpublished manuscript)

Because this is a narrative, sentence Themes frequently refer to the characters (by their names or by pronouns), as the story is about them and their actions. But the author also uses Themes that introduce place (*at school*) and time (*during the summer, for the first couple of weeks apart*), shifting and developing the context of the characters' activities. Other sentence Themes include conjunctions: Here, *but* to introduce a contrast/change (*But during the summer*; *But the emailing*). These Themes are typical of narratives, as they enable the author to maintain a focus on the characters, indicate shifts in time and place, and introduce complications.

The notion of Theme captures the insight that in English, writers use the beginning of a sentence to shape a text, either continuing a previous point or redirecting the text toward a new point. (While Theme is a feature of every clause, in this chapter the focus is on sentence Themes.) With knowledge about Theme, teachers can go beyond naming grammatical structures and help students focus on what different structures are enabling a writer to accomplish. Identifying Themes in a text supports students in recognizing the words that go together to create a meaningful element as a sentence begins, as well as in thinking about what a writer is achieving in making that choice.

While often the Theme is the subject of a sentence, students can look for sentences that begin with something other than a subject to explore how authors make transitions in a story. The use of non-subject Themes in shaping a narrative can be seen in a sequence of Themes from a children's story, *Little Grunt and the Big Egg* by Tomie dePaola (1990):

- Once upon a time, in a big cave, past the volcano on the left,
- One Saturday morning,
- That night,
- But there was
- The next morning,
- That night,
- All of a sudden
- And before you could say Tyrannosaurus Rex,
- And they all lived happily ever after.

We see the fairy tale genre here in the opening and closing lines. Within the tale, the sentence Themes reveal that the story is organized to move through time (*one Saturday morning, that night*, etc.) In addition, Themes introduce two complications, a characteristic of narrative (*But there* was a problem; *All of a sudden*). Resolution of the problem is also signaled by a sentence Theme: *And before you could say Tyrannosaurus Rex,…*.

Themes vary by genre. In procedural texts, the Themes are typically the imperative verb that is a directive to act, for example in recipes or instructions:

Take two cups of sugar…
Screw the bolt onto the board…

In descriptions or simple reports, sentence Themes often stay focused on a particular aspect of the meaning of the text as the author builds up information about the topic, as in this introduction to a text about wildfires:

A raging wildfire is a frightening thing. *Living trees* burn as fast as cardboard boxes in a bonfire. *Flames* race through the treetops, sometimes faster than a person can run, burning at a temperature hot enough to melt steel. *A wildfire* can be a major disaster, capable of destroying hundreds of homes and costing human lives. *But not all fires* are bad. *Fires in nature* can help as well as harm. *A burned forest* allows young plants to begin growing. *And fire* is necessary for some trees, such as sequoias, to release their seeds. *Instead of being an ending*, fire is often a new chapter in the continuing story of the natural world. (From *Wildfires* by Seymour Simon, 1996)

Here, the Themes introduce the notion of *wildfire* and then use related notions (*Living trees, Flames, Wildfires*) to build up the idea presented in the first sentence, that wildfires can be *frightening*. In the middle of the paragraph, however, *But not all fires* shifts the focus. The following Theme, *Fires in nature*, identifies a kind of wildfire that is not bad. This idea is further developed in the sentences introduced by the fire-oriented Themes that follow (*A burned forest, And fire*), each of which introduces a positive effect of wildfires (*can help as well as harm*; *allow young plants to begin growing*; etc.); and the final Theme, *Instead of being an ending*, introduces the main point of the text, to describe how a forest recovers from a fire. Looking across this text and recognizing the contrast that is introduced in the middle of the paragraph can help students interpret and synthesize the information being built up sentence by sentence.

In explanations, what is introduced as new information at the end of a sentence is often distilled and condensed in the Theme of the following sentence. We see this pattern in a text on *Ice Movement* (sentences are numbered for purposes of explanation below):

> (1) *In high mountain areas*, large thicknesses of snow can collect. (2) *This* is compressed by its own weight and hardened. (3) *The compression of the snow* can cause it to form into large bodies of ice. (4) *The weight of the snow and ice* causes the ice to move slowly down the valley. (5) *This moving body of ice* is called a glacier. (6) *The slow but powerful movement of the ice* erodes sediments from the mountains and eventually carves out a large U-shaped valley, which is quite different from a river valley. (7) *The movement of the ice* as it goes downhill also results in cracks, called crevasses, forming in the glacier. (From Heffernan & Learmonth, 1988: 129; cited in Veel, 1998)

Students can notice that the text begins with the Theme *In high mountain areas*, setting up the context in which snow collects. The second sentence begins with *This*, referring back to what has been said in the first sentence. When sentences begin with *This*, *These*, or other demonstratives, readers often need to look back to the prior text to recognize what is being referred to.

Sentence (3) begins a pattern of information development that is common in an explanation. After we read in (2) that snow *is compressed*, the Theme in sentence (3) distills that point in a noun phrase, *The compression of the snow*. Sentence (3) introduces the idea that this creates *large bodies of ice*, which is presented in sentence Theme (4) as *The weight of the snow and ice*. Sentence (4) introduces the notion that the ice *moves*, and then the Themes of (5) *This moving body of ice* and (6) *The ... movement* continue to develop the explanation. Teachers who are alert to this pattern of information flow in explanations can help their students look for text sequences in which concepts are introduced in one sentence and then picked up in the Theme of the following sentence, enabling information to accumulate and develop across a text.

Exploring Themes through close reading activities also supports students in identifying places where a text takes a turn in a new direction. For example, in this primary source from an ancient Chinese historian, used in a seventh-grade social studies class unit on the Silk Road, the text opens with a purpose clause as its initial Theme:

> *To take the shorter desert route*, you have to cross a plain of sand that extends for more than 300 miles. *You* see nothing in any direction but the sky and the sands, without the slightest trace of a road. *Travelers* find nothing to guide them but the bones of men and beasts and the droppings of camels. *During the passage through this wilderness* you hear sounds, sometimes of singing, sometimes of crying. *It has often happened* that travelers have tried to see what those sounds might be and have wandered from their course and been entirely lost. *The sounds* are the voices of spirits and goblins. *For these reasons*, travelers and merchants often prefer the much longer route north of the mountains. (Modified from Ma Duanlin, circa 1300; unpublished curriculum materials)

The author begins by setting up the purpose of the text, to describe the shorter route through the desert. The next Themes are *You* and *Travelers*, the readers that the historian is speaking to through sentences that describe what they will see. Then, a Theme of time orients the reader to what will happen *during the passage*. This introduces a new phase of the text, about the sounds that travelers will experience, and the Theme *It has often happened* identifies the danger that the historian is warning about. Here, we see a brief explanation sequence, as the sentence Theme *The sounds* picks up what has been presented in the previous sentence. Finally, the Theme *For these reasons* refers back to the content of the previous three sentences to move the text to the author's key point, that travelers often prefer the longer route.

Looking at this passage as a whole, teachers can see that it is organized to introduce the dangers of the shorter route and offer an implicit recommendation to take the longer route. By having students identify the Themes, teachers can help them recognize the three main parts of this text, where first they read about the shorter route and then about the sounds, and finally come to the conclusion. This example also illustrates that the organization of a sentence to move from a point of departure toward something new is often echoed across a text as a whole. Here the opening Theme, *To take the shorter desert route*, and the final clause, *travelers and merchants often prefer the much longer route*, give the paragraph as a whole a structure that shows its purpose is to recommend the longer route.

Sentence Themes also often support a writer in presenting an argument. In Dr. Martin Luther King's 1963 *Letter from a Birmingham Jail*, he uses sentence Themes to shape his argument that responds to critics who have opposed his movement:

> *While confined here in the Birmingham city jail*, I came across your recent statement calling our present activities "unwise and untimely." *Seldom, if ever*, do I pause to answer criticism of my work and ideas. *If I* sought to answer all of the criticisms that cross my desk, my secretaries would be engaged in little else in the course of the day, and I would have no time for constructive work. *But since I* feel that you are men of genuine good will and your criticisms are sincerely set forth, I would like to answer your statement in what I hope will be patient and reasonable terms.

Dr. King begins by presenting the time and place from which he writes. His second sentence Theme refers to how unusual it is (*seldom, if ever*) that he would respond to critics, saying what would happen *if* he answered them all. The text then takes a turn (*But*) to give a reason (*since*) for why King (*I*) is answering now.

Later in the letter, Dr. King shapes his response by using the Theme position to foreground his own perspective, moving from the opening *you* to *I* as he develops the argument that responds to the critics:

> *You* deplore the demonstrations that are presently taking place in Birmingham. *But I am sorry* that your statement did not express a similar concern for the conditions that brought the demonstrations into being. *I am sure* that each of you would want to go beyond the superficial social analyst who looks merely at effects, and does not grapple with underlying causes. *I would not hesitate to say* that it is unfortunate that so-called demonstrations are taking place in Birmingham at this time, *but I would say in more emphatic terms* that it is even more unfortunate that the white power structure of this city left the Negro community with no other alternative.

After moving from *you* to *But I am sorry* to respond to the critics' particular point, Dr. King introduces each following sentence/clause with a Theme that underscores his confidence and determination: *I am sure, I would not hesitate to say, but I would say in more emphatic terms*.

Students can recognize the power in this phrasing for framing the argument that King is making in strong and personal terms.

Analyzing Themes gives students opportunities to think about differences in genres (stories, procedures, reports, explanation, arguments) and how they unfold. Exploration of the meaning in sentence Themes supports close reading for understanding, but also raises awareness about language that students could adopt in their writing. In describing the ways that language develops across the school years, Christie (2012) has noted that flexible and varied use of Theme is an important marker of writers' growth and progress. A focus on Theme in the texts they read can support learners in recognizing how this language resource can help them structure their own writing in different genres.

Analyzing Themes with Students

To plan for a focus on Theme, teachers need to analyze the text themselves, identifying the ways that the Themes shape the text and planning the conversation that they will lead as they engage their students in exploration of the structure of a particular text. Theme is a good way to get started with functional grammar, as identifying a Theme just depends on being able to recognize the first meaningful phrase in the sentence. A Theme can be presented in any of the parts of speech: in noun phrases, verb phrases, prepositional phrases, adverbs, or conjunctions. A conjunction does not take up the whole Theme position, so the Theme of a sentence beginning with a conjunction also includes the next meaningful phrase. It is possible to get started with Theme analysis without other technical linguistic metalanguage (*noun*, *verb*, *preposition*, etc.) by just identifying the word or phrase that starts the sentence without naming that structure. But working with Themes also offers contexts where using other linguistic metalanguage to name the structures can be made meaningful, in contrast to activities that ask students to identify noun phrases or other structures out of contexts of meaning.

Students will need to be introduced to the role of Theme in structuring texts, with opportunities to practice identifying it to consider what it means and how that meaning relates to what has come before and what comes next in the text. Table 2.1 offers questions that can be used to explore the meanings presented in Themes of different kinds.

An example: A seventh-grade class is reading a news report about South Africa (Themes in italics below). The teacher wants them to recognize that the paragraph below is organized as an argument, with a claim in the first sentence followed by three sentences that provide evidence for the claim. The last sentence then introduces an alternative claim. Having already introduced the notion of Theme, the teacher has students identify the sentence Themes that present *time* and *contrast*. This helps them recognize the time frame of the article and the meaning of *And yet*.

Table 2.1 Theme analysis

Analyzing how sentences begin

Questions to explore: What comes first in a sentence? How does the writer move from sentence to sentence? Does what is introduced in one sentence get picked up in the Theme of the following sentence? What meanings are built up and developed across the text?

If the Theme is a noun or noun phrase, explore:

- Does the Theme refer to something or someone that has already been introduced into the text or does it introduce something or someone new?

- If the Theme is a pronoun or demonstrative (e.g., *he, they, that,* etc.), what does it refer to?

- If the Theme is a complex noun phrase, what information does it include?

- If the Theme refers to the author of the text, what perspective does it present?

If the Theme is a verb or verb phrase, explore:

- Does the Theme direct the reader to do something? (*Look, Take,...*)

- Does it introduce a question (*Is, Are, Do...?*).

- Does it introduce a dependent clause (e.g., *Coming around the corner...*; *To create an electric circuit...*). How does that clause relate to what is coming next in the text?

If the Theme is a prepositional phrase, adverb, conjunction, or dependent clause, explore:

- What meaning does the Theme introduce? Possible meanings include *time, sequence, location, manner, addition, comparison/contrast, cause, condition, purpose,* and others. How does that meaning relate to what is coming next in the text?

In the 18 years since black-majority rule began and South Africa became a full democracy, its people have made progress. *Many more* now have access to clean water and electricity. *...The racist legislation of apartheid* has been abolished. *The new constitution* is liberal and inspiring.

And yet in other ways South Africa is in a worse state than at any point since 1994. (From *The Economist,* 2012)

The teacher probes for further discussion about the ways the first claim is supported by evidence, generating conversation about the meaning of the Themes *Many more* in the second sentence, *The racist legislation of apartheid* in the third, and *The new constitution* in the fourth, and about how these sentences describe changes that have led to progress. He then asks students to read further to find out what the author is referring to by *in other ways* in the Theme of the last sentence, giving them a frame for reading further in the news article. (For further examples of Theme analysis, see Brown [2009], Fang & Schleppegrell [2008], French [2010], and Schleppegrell [2004, 2009].)

The analysis of Theme gives students an opportunity to look more deeply into the choices an author has made. Having students work together in pairs or small groups to identify Themes can encourage talk about the text and its meanings that further supports reading comprehension. For struggling readers, identifying all the words that go together to make up the Theme can support seeing how English works.

Students can learn to recognize Theme as a language resource that often signals changes in a text's direction or distills information that has already been presented. A focus on Theme can support students in engaging with more challenging content and enable their full participation in grade-appropriate literacy activities. Conscious attention to language and how it works can support students as they encounter different patterns of text organization in their curricular texts.

Conclusion

This chapter has introduced the notion of sentence Theme as a resource for focusing on text structure through an analytic approach that helps learners investigate how an author moves from one sentence to another to build a text. It has illustrated how narratives, procedures, descriptions, explanations, and arguments vary in the typical Themes they present, showing how the choices that authors make in sentence Themes are part of what differentiates genres. Identifying and talking about meaning in Themes can be a first step that even teachers without deep knowledge about language can take to get started in learning more themselves so that they can bring a greater focus to the ways that language works as they interact with their students.

References

Brown, D.W. (2009) *Lessons on Grammar, Code-Switching, and Academic Writing.* Portsmouth, NH: Heinemann.
Christie, F. (2012) *Language Education Throughout the School Years: A Functional Perspective.* Malden, MA: Wiley-Blackwell.
Derewianka, B. (2011) *A New Grammar Companion for Teachers.* Sydney: Primary English Teachers Association.
dePaola, T. (1990) *Little Grunt and the Big Egg.* New York: G.P. Putnam's Sons.
Fang, Z. and Schleppegrell, M.J. (2008) *Reading in Secondary Content Areas: A Language-Based Pedagogy.* Ann Arbor, MI: University of Michigan Press.
French, R. (2010) Primary school children learning grammar: Rethinking the possibilities. In T. Locke (ed.) *Beyond the Grammar Wars: A Resource for Teachers and Students on Developing Language Knowledge in the English/Literacy Classroom* (pp. 206–229). New York: Routledge.
Halliday, M.A.K. (1994) *An Introduction to Functional Grammar* (2nd edn). London: Edward Arnold.
Halliday, M.A.K. (2004) Three aspects of children's language development: Learning language, learning through language, learning about language. In J. Webster (ed.) *The Language of Early Childhood* (Vol. 4; pp. 308–326). London: Continuum.
Heffernan, D.A. and Learmonth, M.S. (1988) *The World of Science: Book One.* Melbourne: Longman Cheshire.
King, M.L., Jr. (1963) *Letter from a Birmingham Jail.* Transcribed from The Martin Luther King, Jr. Research and Education Institute, Stanford University. See https://kinginstitute.stanford.edu/king-papers/documents/letter-birmingham-jail (accessed 28 February 2018).
Ma Duanlin (circa 1300) Unpublished curriculum materials under development by author and colleagues.

Schleppegrell, M.J. (2004) *The Language of Schooling: A Functional Linguistics Perspective.* Mahwah, NJ: Lawrence Erlbaum.

Schleppegrell, M.J. (2009) Grammar for generation 1.5: A focus on meaning. In M. Roberge, M. Siegal and L. Harklau (eds) *Generation 1.5 in College Composition: Teaching Academic Writing to U.S.-Educated Learners of ESL* (pp. 221–234). New York: Routledge.

Simon, S. (1996) *Wildfires.* New York: Harper Collins.

Symons, C. (n.d.) Best Friends. Unpublished manuscript.

The Economist (October 20, 2012) Over the Rainbow. See http://www.economist.com/news/briefing/21564829-it-has-made-progress-becoming-full-democracy-1994-failure-leadership-means (accessed 28 February 2018).

Veel, R. (1998) The greening of school science: Ecogenesis in secondary classrooms. In J.R. Martin and R. Veel (eds) *Reading Science: Critical and Functional Perspectives on Discourses of Science* (pp. 114–151). London: Routledge.

3 What Educators Need to Know About Academic Language: Insights from Recent Research

Paola Uccelli and Emily Phillips Galloway

Readers of this chapter who are middle school teachers are likely to have observed their own students struggling with the language of texts. About three decades ago, Jim Cummins (1980) noted that emergent bilinguals—that is, students learning the language of school as an additional language—often demonstrated proficiency in their new language in conversational settings, but continued to struggle with the language of school texts. Recent evidence shows that academic language is also challenging for many English-proficient students, especially for academically vulnerable students from low-income communities. In fact, our own research, as well as that of others, reveals that English-proficient students display considerable individual differences in academic language proficiency. Attuned to this reality, many educators are concerned with how to support all students to become proficient users of the language of school literacy and learning. The challenge, however, is that while the need to teach academic language is widely recognized, which language skills to teach is less clear.

This chapter begins to answer the question: What do today's educators need to know about academic language? To offer more concrete guidelines as to which skills are worth teaching, we draw from seven years of research on upper elementary and middle school students' school-relevant language skills, work conducted in partnership with educators from large urban districts in the United States. Extending Fillmore and Snow's chapter in this volume, we focus in particular on cross-disciplinary academic language skills—what they are, why they are important, and how to support their development during the upper elementary and middle school years. We identify an array of high-utility, cross-disciplinary language skills that we call Core Academic Language Skills (CALS), which are particularly relevant in the transition from elementary to middle school to support comprehension and learning across content areas. Certainly, CALS do not capture all the language challenges that readers experience with school texts, but making this core array of high-utility language skills visible to educators and researchers constitutes an important step toward designing academic language-focused instruction. On the basis of our findings, we argue that schools run the risk of maintaining and exacerbating the inequalities that exist in the larger society when they do not address variability in students' language skills: Students who are socialized outside of school into the language and literacy practices valued in classrooms will continue to have a better chance of achieving academic success than those who lack these opportunities (Uccelli *et al.*, 2015).

In the next sections, we present four key research-based understandings about academic language learning. We conclude by discussing the implications of these understandings for day-to-day academic language instruction with the hope that educators will find them insightful.

Key Understandings About Academic Language

Our research agenda was inspired by our partners, educators teaching in large linguistically diverse urban districts, who reported that even students who were skilled readers throughout primary school often experienced difficulties in understanding the academic language of middle school texts. Even when students could successfully decode the text and even when the vocabulary words in their texts had been taught, large proportions of students found the language of texts inaccessible. These teachers' reports echoed results from numerous vocabulary interventions, most of which succeeded in increasing students' vocabulary knowledge, yet failed at substantially improving middle schoolers' text comprehension (Elleman *et al.*, 2009). Vocabulary instruction, while essential, has proven insufficient. This is perhaps not surprising if we understand that vocabulary knowledge is most likely a proxy for a larger repertoire of language skills. After all, a skilled reader and writer with a rich vocabulary has also learned how to use and understand these words in complex and concise syntactic structures and to signal logical relations or viewpoints through precise markers. As we discuss below, language proficiency is a comprehensive, dynamic skill set, which includes knowledge of much more than the meanings of single words.

Key understanding #1: Language and reading development continue during adolescence and need to be supported

Aligned with educators' observations, research now shows that native language development, which was once conceptualized as complete after elementary school, continues throughout adolescence and potentially throughout life. Adolescents, in particular, experience substantive language growth as they learn new content through a variety of oral and written texts at school (Nippold, 2007). Beyond new word meanings, adolescents' language growth entails several other domains, such as complex grammar, logical connectives (*nevertheless, consequently*), and markers of an author's viewpoint (*it is extremely unlikely that...; it might be true that...*).

What does this mean for how we understand reading development? For one thing, during the upper elementary and middle school years, students' academic language skills become more important in predicting reading comprehension. As students achieve accuracy and automaticity in "cracking the code," differences between students in word recognition skills decrease and variability in academic language proficiency becomes a primary predictor of reading comprehension (Kieffer *et al.*, 2016; Uccelli *et al.*, 2015). In line with these developmental findings, nearly all U.S. instructional standards today, whether the Common Core State Standards (National Governors Association, 2010) or the Next Generation Science Standards (NGSS, 2013), acknowledge the central role of academic language teaching in supporting reading comprehension and conceptual learning throughout the secondary school years.

These new research findings make clear that the widely held understanding of literacy development as a move from "learning to read" to "reading to learn" conveys only a partial understanding. Even in the earliest grades, students need to read to learn; and, certainly, adolescents continue to learn to read as they encounter increasingly complex texts. Similarly, learning the language of school has been described as the continuous double task of "learning to talk" and "talking to learn" (Wells & Wells, 1984). To reflect the concurrent learning of language and reading across the grades, we can refer to these mutually beneficial processes as "talking-to-learn from texts" and "learning-to-talk with texts." Engaging adolescents in talking about texts allows educators to observe students' strengths in making meaning from text, as well as to uncover which language features might obstruct rather than facilitate comprehension. During these instructional episodes, the goal is twofold: to foster text comprehension and to expand language skill.

Key understanding #2: Academic language proficiency entails knowledge of vocabulary as well as other language structures characteristic of academic texts

Below, we have analyzed a text written for seventh graders to illustrate the recurrent challenges that adolescent students face when reading at school:

Text 1	
Global leaders are concerned because evidence shows that the Earth's temperatures have **increased** in the recent **decades**. MOREOVER, most scientists agree that [it is *extremely likely* that humans are causing most of this problem through [activities that increase **concentrations** of greenhouse gases]].	• academic vocabulary • [complex text] • CONNECTING markers • conceptual anaphor • **nominalizations** • *viewpoint markers*

In addition to the discipline-specific vocabulary (*greenhouse gases, temperatures*) and the general-purpose academic vocabulary (*global, decade, evidence*), there are more hidden language demands in this paragraph. This text, like most academic texts, packs in dense information through complex syntax and complex words, such as nominalizations, nouns created from verbs or adjectives, which tend to be challenging for students (*active* > *activity; concentrate* > *concentration*). Texts also include different expressions to refer to the same idea, events, or participants, making it difficult for readers to keep track of what is being discussed. This is especially the case for conceptual anaphora; readers need to understand that a noun phrase encapsulates a complex idea expressed in a prior sentence (*this problem* = *the Earth's temperatures have increased in recent decades*). Connecting markers (e.g., *moreover*) signal how ideas are related; yet, they are helpful only if readers understand them. Readers also need to pay attention to the subtle ways that writers signal their viewpoints, for example to accentuate or attenuate their claims (*extremely likely*).

The challenges posed by the language in this excerpt might appear to be marginal for meaning-making. However, a quick exercise highlights the importance of these features: First, read Text 1 and answer the question: *Are humans causing the increase in the Earth's temperatures?* Then, read Text 2 and answer the same question. As you will see, despite the minimal differences across texts—one connecting marker (*moreover* v. *nevertheless*) and one viewpoint marker (*likely* v. *unlikely*)—these passages lead to opposite answers ("yes" for Text 1; "no" for Text 2). Clearly, in Text 2 understanding *nevertheless* would be decisive for accurate comprehension. Yet, our data from over 5000 students in Grades 4–8 revealed that the majority of students had not yet learned *nevertheless*; even in eighth grade, only 47% understood this marker. We also found that only a third of middle school students understood *moreover*.

> **Text 2**
> Global leaders are concerned because evidence shows that the Earth's temperatures have increased in the recent decades. **NEVERTHELESS**, most scientists agree that it is **extremely unlikely** that humans are causing most of this problem through activities that increase concentrations of greenhouse gases.
>
> Are humans causing the increase in the Earth's temperatures?

Our research has been dedicated to testing the types of skills illustrated in the above texts, which we refer to as the CALS. CALS are defined as a set of language skills that correspond to linguistic features prevalent in academic texts found across content area classrooms, yet infrequent in informal conversations. In the words of our teacher/researcher collaborator, Melanie Allen, "CALS is the name we use for a group of skills that students need in order to understand complex academic text, even though they don't necessarily need them for everyday conversations." As shown in Table 3.1, CALS include skills in seven domains.

The foregoing definition of CALS contrasts with other characterizations of academic language in two main ways (Nagy & Townsend, 2012). First, the focus is not on general language development, but on the specific language skills that support school reading. Second, instead of discipline-specific skills, CALS are cross-disciplinary skills of high utility that can be systematically scaffolded across content areas.

Table 3.1 Domains and skills measured by the CALS Instrument

CALS domain	Skills measured
Unpacking dense information	Skill in comprehending and using complex words and complex sentences that facilitate concise communication (e.g., nominalizations, embedded clauses, expanded noun phrases).
Connecting ideas logically	Skill in comprehending and using connecting markers prevalent in academic texts to signal relationships between ideas (e.g., *consequently, on the one hand … on the other hand*).
Tracking participants and ideas	Skill in identifying or producing terms or phrases used to refer to the same participants or themes throughout an academic text (e.g., *Water evaporates at 100 degrees Celsius. This process …*).
Organizing analytic texts	Skill in organizing analytic texts according to conventional academic structures, especially argumentative texts (e.g., thesis, argument, counterargument, conclusion) and paragraph-level structures (e.g., compare/contrast; problem/solution).
Understanding metalinguistic vocabulary	Skill in understanding or expressing precise meanings, in particular, in using language to make thinking and reasoning visible, known as metalinguistic vocabulary (e.g., *hypothesis, generalization, argument*).
Understanding a writer's viewpoint	Skill in understanding or using markers that signal a writer's viewpoint, especially epistemic stance markers, those that signal a writer's degree of certainty in relation to a claim (e.g., *certainly; it is unlikely that*).
Recognizing academic language	Skill in recognizing more academic language when contrasted with more colloquial language in communicative contexts where academic language is expected (e.g., *more academic v. more colloquial noun definitions*).

Key understanding #3: Academic language skills vary widely within a single classroom. Both emerging bilinguals and English proficient students require support to learn academic language

A particularly interesting development is the realization that the construct of academic language proficiency is relevant for students other than emerging bilingual learners. Quantitative studies that measure language and reading skills (e.g., Geva & Farnia, 2012; LaRusso *et al.*, 2016) and empirical studies that assess academic vocabulary (e.g., Lesaux *et al.*, 2012) and academic language (Uccelli *et al.*, 2015) reveal that the language demands of reading school texts also pose challenges to English proficient students. Thus, all students are English learners, or more broadly, all students continue to learn the language of school (in whatever language they are instructed at school). In other words, learning at school entails constantly expanding skills and practices regarding not only academic content but also language.

As would be expected, academic language proficiency, on average, is higher in students in the upper grades (Uccelli & Phillips Galloway, 2016). Yet, at the same time, individual differences within the same grade are substantial, with a few fourth graders demonstrating levels of academic language proficiency higher than the average sixth grader (Uccelli *et al.*, 2015). The variability within grade is perhaps most evident when we examine the CALS-Instrument (CALS-I) scores for all students attending one urban middle school (Figure 3.1). In this unorthodox figure produced from our CALS-I data, each line represents the CALS score of an individual student. Longer lines demonstrate higher levels of CALS proficiency. The jagged appearance of this figure communicates a central message about academic language proficiency: Sitting shoulder to shoulder in any classroom are students with starkly varying levels of academic language proficiency.

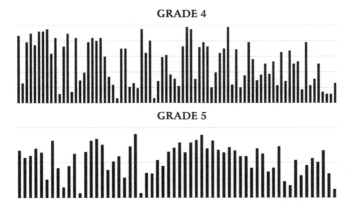

Figure 3.1 CALS individual scores per grade

Key understanding #4: Instruction needs to empower students' voices and welcome out-of-school ways of using language. Young learners whose perspectives and ways of using language are heard and taken seriously will embrace the opportunity to continue to learn

An unintentional result of academic language instruction can be the devaluing of students' home language resources, especially if their home language differs significantly from the language of school. Societal language ideologies focused on correctness are insidious and easily internalized by students. In our interviews with middle graders, we found that students tended to qualify the language of school as "correct," "good," or "better" than the language used in informal conversations (Phillips Galloway et al., 2015). Students also shared that their motivations for using the language of school were to impress others, appear smart, or garner favor from adults. Somewhat surprisingly, almost no student referred to the usefulness of the language learned at school to communicate more precisely. Furthermore, not a single student referred to academic language as a helpful tool to make sense of one's own experience or to critically process or contest others' ideas.

Instructional Implications

Promoting knowledge of CALS

For educators, the unequal distribution of CALS across students demands pedagogies that support those who demonstrate low levels of CALS, while simultaneously stimulating their peers with higher levels of CALS to further hone these skills. CALS teaching requires classroom-level attention, especially in contexts where many students demonstrate low levels of CALS. A rich classroom language learning environment designed to support academic language learning for all provides students with opportunities to engage with complex ideas by participating in peer-to-peer talk and classroom discussions scaffolded by a classroom teacher, with ample opportunities for all learners to produce, practice, and expand their language skills orally and in writing.

We know that interventions focused on text-based discussions have been shown to bolster text comprehension in middle school classrooms (Murphy et al., 2009). Among other factors, a not-so-secret ingredient of the success of this approach may be that it requires the recurrent use of academic language. Teachers themselves provide an important model for academic language use. In contrast to the number of studies that examine the influence of parental language inputs, the research examining the impact of teachers' language is scarce. Recent studies, though, have found that teachers who produce more diverse vocabulary and complex syntax have students with higher language proficiency (Gámez & Lesaux, 2012).

Moreover, framing interesting questions around purposefully selected topics and texts that require the use of complex language in discussion compels both teachers and students to use this language for sharing complex ideas. Pedagogies such as discussion-based approaches that make academic language visible through a cycle of "Read about it, Talk about it, Write about it" seem particularly efficacious (e.g., Word Generation program [http://wordgen.serpmedia.org/]; Snow et al., 2009).

Educators may wonder why we do not simply advocate for immersive reading of text—where academic language is most likely found. It has been estimated that during a typical academic year, students acquire between 1000 (Goulden et al., 1990) and 3000 words (Nagy & Herman, 1987). While text exposure has long been considered a critical mechanism underlying this language learning (Stanovich & Cunningham, 1993), independent reading might not be as effective for less-proficient adolescent readers. Learning language from grade-level text is very challenging for students who cannot understand the text. That is why a multipronged approach is necessary, one that exposes students to language via speech and print, and that scaffolds understanding and language skills through text-based discussion. Thus, there is a need for professional development that emphasizes the centrality of language, together with instructional materials systematically designed to intentionally teach academic language and provide students with plenty of opportunities for meaningful text-based discussions and writing, in order to provide teachers with the support they require for the urgent and complex task of scaffolding adolescents' language and literacy learning (Lesaux et al., 2014; Snow et al., 2009).

Promoting awareness of CALS

Helping students acquire academic language is not simply about teaching skills—it is also about heightening students' awareness of academic language itself. Discussing the language of a text demands that learners apply knowledge about academic language and use academic language resources.

Numerous studies examine the cultivation of metalinguistic awareness in K-12 students, often second language learners. Mostly inspired by systemic functional linguistics (SFL), qualitative studies have explored how teaching and discussing linguistic terminology can heighten learners' attention to language and support their text comprehension (e.g., Berry, 2010; Brisk & Zisselsberger, 2010; de Oliveira, 2016; Schleppegrell, 2011). Because SFL conceptualizes academic language proficiency as register-specific and as the consequence of having had many opportunities to use the language of school, the instructional focus is squarely on creating chances for learners to use academic language. SFL-inspired instruction aims to help developing readers and writers recognize that meaning is constructed through the language choices made by language users (Schleppegrell, 2013, 2016, this volume).

Our own work in this area offers an additional entry point to talking about language with students. In addition to using promising interventions focused on teaching linguistic terms, eliciting students' own metalanguage and reflections about language through discussions about contrasting pairs of texts (typically one more colloquial and another more academic, but many other contrasts are possible) leads to insightful and engaging interactions. Our studies of middle graders' reflections discovered students' own apt—even if non-technical—terms to reflect about academic language features and expectations (Phillips Galloway *et al.*, 2015). Multi-party discussions in which students build on the language of peers appear to be particularly useful contexts for making the hidden curriculum of academic language learning visible to students. These discussions offer an entry point for teachers, allowing them to gradually build the precise metalanguage that a class needs on the basis of what students already know. In these dialogical spaces, teachers can expand academic language resources as choices to be used flexibly and reflectively, with language users adhering to conventional uses, but also departing from them to communicate their ideas and perspectives. In this way, students' out-of-school language resources are welcomed and valued, while societal language hierarchies are explicitly counteracted. A fundamental pedagogical ingredient entails making explicit to students that academic language resources are also useful for making sense of their own experiences and for contesting others' ideas.

Anticipating students' challenges with the language of text

In a dual language public school in the Northeast, our teacher/ researcher collaborator, Melanie Allen, worked with the results from her fifth- and sixth-grade students' CALS assessments to incorporate the CALS skills included in the broader construct into her English language arts and social studies combined curricular unit. Table 3.2 shows the six questions that Melanie asked herself before preparing for class. She found these questions helpful to anticipate her students' challenges with text. In the Appendix, we provide a table with additional CALS-guided questions that our partner teacher used to prepare for text discussions with students.

Conclusion

This chapter started with a question: What do today's educators need to know about academic language? We end by sharing a final reflection: The ability to express oneself flexibly and freely, as well as to access

Table 3.2 CALS text-preview routines

Will my students have difficulty understanding
(1) This type of text? Is the text organized in a structure that my students are familiar with?
(2) The complex words in this text?
(3) Sentences that differ from the way they usually talk or write (word order, length of sentence)?
(4) Connecting words that indicate relations between ideas?
(5) How to track ideas—or people—in the text that are referred to in different ways?
(6) Words or phrases that reveal the author's attitude or level of conviction?

the words of one's contemporaries or the voices of the past through text, constitute basic human rights. We remind all educators, including ourselves, that teachers can exert a significant impact on students' lives by cultivating language, by listening, by scaffolding language, and by socializing learners into reflective and critical language users.

Acknowledgments

We would like to thank the students who participated in our studies, as well as our close collaborators: Christopher L. Barr, Alejandra Meneses, Gladys Aguilar, Melanie Allen, Christina Dobbs, and Emilio Sánchez. The research reported here was supported by the Institute of Education Sciences, U.S. Department of Education, through Grant R305F100026 to the Strategic Education Research Partnership (SERP) as part of the Reading for Understanding Research Initiative, and by a grant from the Observatorio de la lengua española y las culturas hispánicas en los Estados Unidos, Instituto Cervantes at Harvard University. All opinions expressed are those of the authors and do not represent the views of the institute, the U.S. Department of Education, or the Instituto Cervantes.

References

Berry, R. (2010) *Terminology in English Language Teaching: Nature and Use* (Vol. 93). New York: Peter Lang.

Brisk, M.E. and Zisselsberger, M. (2010) We've let them in on the secret. In T. Lucus (ed.) *Teacher Preparation for Linguistically Diverse Classrooms: A Resource for Teacher Educators* (pp. 111–127). New York: Routledge.

Cummins, J. (1980) The cross-lingual dimensions of language proficiency: Implications for bilingual education and the optimal age issue. *TESOL Quarterly* 14 (2), 175–187.

de Oliveira, L.C. (2016) A language-based approach to content instruction (LACI) for English language learners: Examples from two elementary teachers. *International Multilingual Research Journal* 10 (3), 217–231.

Elleman, A.M., Lindo, E.J., Morphy, P. and Compton, D.L. (2009) The impact of vocabulary instruction on passage-level comprehension of school-age children: A meta-analysis. *Journal of Research on Educational Effectiveness* 2 (1), 1–44.

Gámez, P.B. and Lesaux, N.K. (2012) The relation between exposure to sophisticated and complex language and early-adolescent English-only and language minority learners' vocabulary. *Child Development* 83 (4), 1316–1331.

Geva, E. and Farnia, F. (2012) Developmental changes in the nature of language proficiency and reading fluency paint a more complex view of reading comprehension in ELL and EL1. *Reading and Writing* 25 (8), 1819–1845.

Goulden, R., Nation, P. and Read, J. (1990) How large can a receptive vocabulary be? *Applied Linguistics* 11 (4), 341–363.

Kieffer, M.J., Petscher, Y., Proctor, C.P. and Silverman, R.D. (2016) Is the whole greater than the sum of its parts? Modeling the contributions of language comprehension skills to reading comprehension in the upper elementary grades. *Scientific Studies of Reading* 20 (6), 436–454.

LaRusso, M., Kim, H.Y., Selman, R., Uccelli, P., Dawson, T., Jones, S. and Snow, C. (2016) Contributions of academic language, perspective taking, and complex reasoning to deep reading comprehension. *Journal of Research on Educational Effectiveness* 9 (2), 201–222.

Lesaux, N.K., Harris, J.R. and Sloane, P. (2012) Adolescents' motivation in the context of an academic vocabulary intervention in urban middle school classrooms. *Journal of Adolescent & Adult Literacy* 56 (3), 231–240.

Lesaux, N.K., Kieffer, M.J., Kelley, J.G. and Harris, J.R. (2014) Effects of academic vocabulary instruction for linguistically diverse adolescents: Evidence from a randomized field trial. *American Educational Research Journal* 51 (6), 1159–1194.

Murphy, P.K., Wilkinson, I.A., Soter, A.O., Hennessey, M.N. and Alexander, J.F. (2009) Examining the effects of classroom discussion on students' comprehension of text: A meta-analysis. *Journal of Educational Psychology* 101 (3), 740–764.

Nagy, W.E. and Herman, P.A. (1987) Breadth and depth of vocabulary knowledge: Implications for acquisition and instruction. In M.G. McKeown and M.E. Curtis (eds) *The Nature of Vocabulary Acquisition* (pp. 19–37). New York: Taylor & Francis.

Nagy, W. and Townsend, D. (2012) Words as tools: Learning academic vocabulary as language acquisition. *Reading Research Quarterly* 47 (1), 91–108.

National Governors Association (2010) *Common Core State Standards*. Washington, DC: National Governors Association Center for Best Practices and the Council of Chief State School Officers.

NGSS (2013) *Next Generation Science Standards: For States, by States*. Washington, DC: The National Academies Press.

Nippold, M.A. (2007) *Later Language Development: School-age Children, Adolescents, and Young Adults*. Austin, TX: Pro-ed.

Phillips Galloway, E.P., Stude, J. and Uccelli, P. (2015) Adolescents' metalinguistic reflections on the academic register in speech and writing. *Linguistics and Education* 31, 221–237.

Schleppegrell, M.J. (2011) Supporting disciplinary learning through language analysis: Developing historical literacy. In F. Christie and K. Maton (eds) *Disciplinarity: Functional Linguistic and Sociological Perspectives* (pp. 197–216). New York: Bloomsbury Publishing.

Schleppegrell, M.J. (2013) The role of metalanguage in supporting academic language development. *Language Learning* 63 (1), 153–170.

Schleppegrell, M.J. (2016) Content-based language teaching with functional grammar in the elementary school. *Language Teaching* 49 (1), 116–128.

Snow, C.E., Lawrence, J.F. and White, C. (2009) Generating knowledge of academic language among urban middle school students. *Journal of Research on Educational Effectiveness* 2 (4), 325–344.

Stanovich, K.E. and Cunningham, A.E. (1993) Where does knowledge come from? Specific associations between print exposure and information acquisition. *Journal of Educational Psychology* 85 (2), 211–229.

Uccelli, P. and Phillips Galloway, E. (2017) Academic language across content areas: Lessons from an innovative assessment and from students' reflections about language. *Journal of Adolescent & Adult Literacy* 60 (4), 395–404.

Uccelli, P., Phillips Galloway, E., Barr, C.D., Meneses, A. and Dobbs, C.L. (2015) Beyond vocabulary: Exploring cross-disciplinary academic-language proficiency and its association with reading comprehension. *Reading Research Quarterly* 50 (3), 337–356.

Wells, G. and Wells, J. (1984) Learning to talk and talking to learn. *Theory into Practice* 23 (3), 190–197.

Appendix

Table A.1 CALS-guided questions for preparing for text discussions with students

CALS domain	Skills	Examples	"Look fors"	CALS text analysis questions
Complex words	Understanding complex words	Nominalizations: *invasion* *durability*	Words ending in *-ion, -ility,- tion, -ty*	What does this word mean? Do you know other words with the same beginning?
Complex sentences	Understanding complex sentences	Expanded noun phrases, center-embedded clauses:	Long or packed sentences, commas, semicolons, dashes	Why is the information contained between the commas important? What is the author telling us in this sentence?
Connecting ideas	Understanding words that connect ideas	*consequently* *in conclusion*	Connecting words	What does this word tell us about how the ideas are related? Do you know another word that means the same?
Tracking participants and themes	Tracking referents through a text	*Water evaporates at 100 degrees Celsius. This process...*	Pronouns	Who or what is the author referring to here? How do you know?
Organizing analytic texts	Organizing argumentative texts	*Some think ... Others think...*	Non-narrative text structures	Ask students if they can anticipate what might follow in a paragraph that starts with ...
Understanding metalinguistic vocabulary	Understanding words that refer to thinking and reasoning	*hypothesis* *inference*	Words that refer to reasoning steps or qualities	What does this word mean in this context?
Interpreting writers' viewpoints	Interpreting words that signal a writer's attitude or level of certainty about a claim	*presumably* *conclusively*	Words that signal how an author feels about a claim or how certain he/she is about the claim	How does the author feel about x? How do you know? Is the author convinced or a bit unsure about the claim?

4 Language and Instruction: Research-Based Lesson Planning and Delivery for English Learner Students

Sarah C. K. Moore, Lindsey A. Massoud, and Joanna Duggan

In their chapter, Fillmore and Snow (this volume) discuss the important role of teachers' knowledge about language to support students' learning of both content and academic language. The authors note recent advancements in the field related to academic language theory, research, assessments, and instructional practices. To appropriately address the needs of English learners, teachers must be equipped to conduct instruction and adapt curriculum to ensure subject-matter content learning and English language development, and, when at all possible, native language maintenance. Doing so requires assessment of students' knowledge, skills, and proficiencies, as well as an understanding of their backgrounds. This information should be used carefully in lesson planning to support successful lesson delivery and, ultimately, students' academic growth and development.

In this chapter, we outline the recommendations that we give to pre- and in-service teachers on planning and delivering lessons appropriately adapted to meet the language and content learning needs of English learners. We present these suggestions in relation to four key dimensions of planning lessons for English learners: developing language objectives, integrating native language instructional supports, helping students access complex text, and building students' argumentation knowledge and skills. Each domain directly links to considerations for standards-aligned instruction and, in particular, to the Common Core State Standards and other college- and career-readiness standards. These foci for lesson planning are informed by educational linguistics and grounded in research and theory related to teaching English learners. Teachers who take these four areas into account as they plan standards-aligned lessons for English learners will increase their capacity to serve English learners as they hone their practice.

Developing Language Objectives

Planning lessons in today's educational environment centrally involves orientation to standards. Recent large-scale, top-down efforts have focused on ensuring that teachers in the country's schools are equipped with the background knowledge necessary for developing content objectives to guide their lessons (Eisner, 1967/1983) and implementing standards-aligned content instruction (Porter *et al.*, 2012).

In order for teachers to plan lessons that support English learners' development of content knowledge, they must also consider and explicitly identify the language demands embedded in the curriculum and instruction they are delivering. Just as content area standards drive content objectives, language objectives may derive from language standards. However, because certification processes in the majority of states do not involve teacher preparation associated with teaching English learners (Education Commission of the States, 2014; Sutcher *et al.*, 2016), many teachers may not be familiar with and thus not use English language development standards (Samson & Collins, 2012). The English language development standards most widely used in this country are from the WIDA Consortium (https://www.wida.us/membership/states/index.aspx). States not participating in this consortium are part of the ELPA21 Consortium or they have developed and adopted their own standards for English language development.

When crafting language objectives for a lesson, teachers should take into account the language skills that students will need to understand the lesson's content and underlying concepts, including the language that the teacher or text will use to convey core content and concepts. A second consideration is the language required for students to communicate their understanding of the content and concepts. Another key concern in developing language objectives is to include the four language domains: reading, writing, listening, and speaking. Across a unit of instruction (though perhaps not a particular lesson), all four domains must be integrated into lessons and specifically noted in language objectives so that students can develop both oral and written English language skills. Evidence suggests that strong oral language skills support literacy development (August & Shanahan, 2006). Productive language objectives might read like this: Students will be able to write a paragraph describing the zones of geography in Virginia, and students will be able to discuss the zones of geography in Virginia with peers. Receptive objectives might include these: Students will be able to read a short text about the zones of geography in Virginia, and students will be able to understand a recorded description of Virginia's Tidewater region.

A common misstep in the development of language objectives for lessons with English learners involves over-emphasis on vocabulary and neglect of other critical, complex, language phenomena in a lesson. This point is well made by Fillmore and Snow (this volume) in their example of a text about electricity. They note that the teacher focuses on "both new words and new structures in the context" and that she "extracts student observations about the function of the elements of the sentence, rather than focusing on disembodied forms ... or isolated grammatical structures (p. 11)."

Setting language objectives may also involve considerations such as English learners' demographics (e.g., the language[s] they speak at home, their age, or how long they have been in the United States) and English proficiency levels, as well as students' specific linguistic needs. Thus, teachers designing language objectives are acting in some ways as evaluators, because they must assess students' linguistic needs and knowledge in order to pinpoint what language should be addressed in the lesson.

The Sheltered Instruction Observation Protocol (SIOP) model, a well-known approach to sheltering instruction, calls for specifying both content and language objectives for each lesson and then laying out strategies for addressing them (Echevarría *et al.*, 2017). In thinking about strategies for reaching the lesson objectives, teachers are urged to target both learning strategies and teaching strategies. An example of a teaching strategy is employing scaffolds to make the lesson content accessible to English learners. Learning strategies include equipping students with tools, clues, information, and tactics they can use to decode text and understand spoken language and content. Another example of a learning strategy, one that leverages a student's native language, would be to use knowledge of language structure, such as the fact that a Spanish noun ending in *–idad* almost always has an English cognate that ends in *–ity* (see Fillmore & Snow, this volume).

In sum, teachers developing lessons for English learners need to know about English language proficiency standards and the central role these should play in lesson planning. To address these standards, teachers need to know how to write objectives that specifically target language skills, which means being able to identify the language that students will need in order to both comprehend the lesson's content and express their understanding of it.

Integrating Native Language Supports

Paying explicit attention to using students' native language skills is an essential dimension of planning. There is a strong research base supporting the positive benefits of bilingualism (Bialystok, 2011; Ortega, 2008; Romaine, 1995) and the effectiveness of bilingual and dual language immersion program models for the instruction of English learners. Students in bilingual or dual language immersion programs, where students learn through and develop both first and second languages, experience long-term academic and linguistic advantages compared with English learners in English as a second language or English-only programs (Greene, 1999; McField & McField, 2014; Rolstad *et al.*, 2005), suggesting that first language development supports learning in a second language. In fact, in a seminal study conducted by Thomas and Collier (2002), students in dual language immersion settings outperformed their peers in transitional and developmental bilingual programs on academic assessments in English, Spanish, and math.

Strong native language literacy skills support the development of second language literacy skills (August & Shanahan, 2006). Studies show that the development of reading comprehension skills and their underlying processes in the native language is significantly associated with reading in the second language (Genesee *et al.*, 2006). Additionally, evidence suggests a facilitative effect for English learners' writing skills, in that skills developed in the native language related to the writing process can also be applied in second language writing (Genesee *et al.*, 2006).

Teachers should know that they must, when possible, complement the instruction of core content in English with additional supports through the integration of students' native languages. Wright (2015) and Freeman and Freeman (2001) propose strategies and activities for incorporating native language supports in the classroom. Examples include conducting preview-view-review activities in the native language; allowing students to respond in their native language during oral discussion; allowing students to conduct pre-writing of first drafts in their native language; displaying students' languages on posters, signs, or labels within the classroom; creating and maintaining a library rich with authentic, high-quality multilingual and multicultural books; providing students with access to bilingual glossaries or dictionaries; reading aloud books that reinforce classroom content in students' native languages; using language buddies, in which English learners who share a native language work together in pairs (while avoiding concurrent translation); and inviting family and/or community members to visit the class. Teachers might also consider identifying and employing technology-based native language supports accessible through the internet (e.g., the Multilingual Children's Book Library), apps (e.g., FluentU), social media (e.g., Pinterest), or other outlets.

Through strategic and planful lesson development that involves the integration of English learners' native languages, teachers will better promote students' academic success, English language development, and native language maintenance, with the intention of supporting students in becoming fully bilingual and biliterate. Classrooms should welcome ethnic, linguistic, and cultural diversity by fostering pride in bilingualism that allows students to "not have to choose between worlds but ... live successfully in both" (Freeman & Freeman, 2001: 177).

Helping Students Access Complex Text

Learning to handle complex text is a particular challenge for English learners, one that teachers can address systematically. In order to plan lessons in which students are supported in reading complex text, teachers first need to understand what makes text complex and realize that mere instruction of vocabulary unfamiliar to students does not suffice (although it may indeed help). A range of textual features may make a text difficult for students in addition to unfamiliar vocabulary, including complex grammatical structures (e.g., information-packed noun phrases) and textual themes and discursive structures that are typical of academic writing in the United States or that are unfamiliar to students for any number of reasons.

However, rather than focusing solely on the complexity of the text that students are reading, we suggest that as teachers plan lessons, they focus on text difficulty and accessibility, prioritizing the needs of their students and examining the interactions between students and text. The following excerpt describes the difference:

> We ... reserve the term complexity to describe lexical, syntactic, and discourse-level features of text. Text difficulty can be understood as challenges to comprehension performance experienced by specific readers engaging with specific texts under specific conditions. We use a third term, accessibility, to describe instructional scaffolds teachers provide to increase a given group of students' likelihood of comprehending a specific text. (Bunch *et al.*, 2014: 536)

When planning lessons, teachers must take into account textual complexity insofar as it may impact text difficulty. Once challenging parts of text have been identified, teachers should determine how they might increase accessibility through use of appropriate instructional strategies.

Some factors that impact the difficulty of a text for a particular student include the student's English language proficiency, literacy in the home language(s), background knowledge, reading strategies, and reading engagement, among other potential factors (Bunch *et al.*, 2014). Thus, when teachers assist students in accessing complex text, it is important that they situate this linguistic activity in a broader context, recognizing features of the text itself, as well as how this language may relate to individual students' backgrounds and abilities.

Although some educators advocate for simplifying complex texts for English learners, this approach restricts their access to the academic language they need to learn, and it may even make the texts more confusing and unclear for readers (Fillmore & Snow, this volume). Furthermore, language learning opportunities should not divorce language form and function: Students need access to language in context, in its "native habitat," so to speak. Addressing form and function together can facilitate students' learning of both language and content, since language forms are connected with, and serve to communicate, the ideologies and approaches inherent in different disciplines (Schleppegrell, 2004). Teachers must understand how to scaffold learning opportunities to afford English learners access to grade-level texts, including, for example, the approach to analyzing "juicy sentences" described in Chapter 1 as well as in more detail in "What does text complexity mean for English learners and language minority students?" (Fillmore & Fillmore, 2013). Students who have learned ways to approach complex text should have opportunities to dig into academic texts. These experiences will help them to understand the relationships between the ideas conveyed in the text and, by extension, help them build the academic language skills needed for success in school and beyond.

Planning activities to help students engage deeply with complex text should involve incorporating the four language domains. Zwiers (2014) incorporates them in variations on read-aloud, such as "comprehend-aloud," which can be used to model for English learners how a proficient reader comprehends a text, including how language and content are related in conveying the message. The students can then read another portion of the text in pairs or groups, following the teacher's model, and take notes on the text using a graphic organizer. We have worked with many teachers on implementing another activity for students' engagement with complex text, called Generating Interactions between Schemata and Text (GIST) (Herrell & Jordan, 2012), which involves students' discussing and clarifying meaning, while generating a concise summary of the reading assignment. These activities involve all four language domains by incorporating reading of a text, listening and speaking with peers and the teacher as they aim to understand the text, and writing about the text.

When planning lessons in which students will engage with complex text, teachers must know what makes texts difficult for students. Based on this awareness, they can make texts more accessible through incorporating methods that shelter content, while also engaging students in language development.

Building Argumentation Skills

As Fillmore and Snow (this volume) point out, the recent shift toward college- and career-readiness standards includes a movement away from summarizing texts and toward constructing arguments based on evidence. Academic argumentation may sometimes be viewed as intrinsically logical. However, when we look at argument structures across cultural contexts, it is clear that there are many ways to make an argument; argument structures are culturally situated and variable across contexts (Fillmore & Snow, this volume). Thus, English learners may need explicit instruction in the argument style expected in U.S. schools, including the interlocutors with whom one may argue, the language forms that can be used, the types of evidence considered valid, how oral argumentation contrasts with written argumentation, and so forth.

As a starting point for planning lessons that engage students in academic argumentation, teachers first need to recognize the skills in argumentation that students bring to the classroom. Teachers should be able to acknowledge and understand the everyday argumentation in which students are already proficient, either in English or their home language (Berland & Reiser, 2009; Bricker & Bell, 2011). Students' implicit understanding and use of claims and evidence in everyday life can be used as a springboard for guiding further understanding and the production of academic argumentation appropriate to the disciplines in which they are working. The language used to convey arguments in academic and discipline-specific settings and the ways of identifying appropriate evidence in these different contexts may be new to them. As Duguay *et al.* (2013: 5) point out, "Students should be made explicitly aware of the different forms of argumentation appropriate to each academic discipline, the process of building and exchanging arguments respectfully within the classroom, and the language embedded in each stage of this process."

It is valuable for teachers to understand how language forms function to convey the ideologies and ways of knowing typical of different content areas. Citing Duschl (2008), Ryu and Sandoval (2012: 490) state, "argumentation ... is a particular social practice, its discursive features grounded in particular epistemic frameworks about what counts as claims, data, warrants, and so forth." The language of argumentation conveys what is valued in a particular discipline, and teachers who are able to recognize this connection can better guide English learners in creating discipline-specific arguments and help them access target language and content. For example, what is appropriate evidence varies across disciplines: In history, primary sources count; in science, data such as measurements matter; while in math, proof of calculations signifies validity. Teachers should know how to identify both what counts as evidence and the linguistic structures used to convey this evidence as justification for a claim. They should facilitate students' construction of arguments that are convincing and appropriate within their specific contexts.

There are also, of course, differences in the language patterns of oral and written academic argumentation. Providing opportunities for students to engage in argumentative discourse, including interaction around student-generated key questions, can play an important role in students' production of academic argumentation (Chin & Osborne, 2010). In planning instructional supports to help students gain access to the language of academic argumentation, we have worked with teachers to increase scaffolding of these forms by providing sentence frames and examples of ways to express different argumentative functions, such as stating a claim (e.g., "It is clear that ...," "I believe that ..."), providing evidence (e.g., "... because ...," "Our evidence is ..."), and stating counterarguments (e.g., "I disagree because ...," "On the other hand ..."). Different types of resources can be provided to students for oral discussions and for writing argumentative essays, as appropriate. Recent research shows strong evidence that integrating English learners' native language for discussion of content-based topics, prior to and as part of the writing process, is beneficial for improving their academic argumentative writing in English (Ahmadian *et al.*, 2016; González-Howard & McNeill, 2016).

Teachers who successfully engage students in learning academic argumentation skills must acknowledge the skills that students bring to the classroom, be able to identify the discursive structures that are appropriate for argumentation in the content areas, understand how these discursive structures relate to ideologies and values within the target discipline, and provide scaffolds for students—including sentence frames in English, the incorporation of all four language domains, and use of students' home languages.

Conclusion

In this chapter, we have addressed four areas related to effective lesson planning for English learners: integrating language objectives, providing native language supports, deconstructing complex text, and building argumentation skills. Becoming expert in these areas will contribute to successful instruction that simultaneously addresses both language and content for English learners. Once teachers are familiar with the characteristics of each domain, why each is important for teaching English learners, and how this foundational knowledge should be applied in practice, teachers will be well equipped to plan lessons that shelter and support English learners in meeting college- and career-readiness standards. They will support students' access to core content and English language development, and promote and celebrate the maintenance of students' native languages, with the goal of achieving full biliteracy, regardless of the primary medium of instruction.

References

Ahmadian, M., Pouromid, S. and Nickkhah, M. (2016) Improving the quality of second language writing by first language use. *Theory and Practice in Language Studies* 6 (4), 767–775.

August, D. and Shanahan, T. (eds) (2006) *Developing Literacy in Second-Language Learners: Report of the National Literacy Panel on Language-Minority Children and Youth*. Mahwah, NJ: Lawrence Erlbaum.

Berland, L.K. and Reiser, B.J. (2009) Making sense of argumentation and explanation. *Science Education* 93 (1), 26–55.

Bialystok, E. (2011) Reshaping the mind: The benefits of bilingualism. *Canadian Journal of Experimental Psychology/Revue canadienne de psychologie expérimentale* 65 (4), 229–235. See http://dx.doi.org/10.1037/a0025406 (accessed 6 March 2018).

Bricker, L.A. and Bell, P. (2011) Argumentation and reasoning in life and in school: Implications for the design of school science learning environments. In M.S. Khine (ed.) *Perspectives on Scientific Argumentation: Theory, Practice, and Research* (pp. 117–134). New York: Springer.

Bunch, G.C., Walqui, A. and Pearson, P.D. (2014) Complex text and new common standards in the United States: Pedagogical implications for English learners. *TESOL Quarterly* 48 (3), 533–559.

Chin, C. and Osborne, J. (2010) Students' questions and discursive interaction: Their impact on argumentation during collaborative group discussions in science. *Journal of Research in Science Teaching* 47 (7), 883–908.

Duguay, A., Massoud, L., Tabaku, L., Himmel, J. and Sugarman, J. (2013) *Implementing the Common Core for English Learners: Responses to Common Questions* (Practitioner Brief). Washington, DC: Center for Applied Linguistics.

Duschl, R.A. (2008) Science education in 3-part harmony: Balancing conceptual, epistemic, and social goals. *Review of Research in Education* 32, 268–291.

Echevarría, J., Vogt, M.E. and Short, D.J. (2017) *Making Content Comprehensible for English Learners: The SIOP Model* (5th edn). New York: Pearson.

Education Commission of the States (2014, November) What ELL Training, If Any, Is Required of General Classroom Teachers? See http://ecs.force.com/mbdata/mbquestNB2?rep=ELL1415 (accessed 6 March 2018).

Eisner, E. (1967/1983) Educational objectives: Help or hindrance. *American Journal of Education* 91 (4), 549–560.

Fillmore, L.W. and Fillmore, C.J. (2013) What does text complexity mean for English learners and language minority students? Understanding Language, Stanford University School of Education, Stanford, CA. See http://ell.stanford.edu/sites/default/files/pdf/academic-papers/06-LWF%20CJF%20Text%20Complexity%20FINAL_0.pdf (accessed 6 March 2018).

Freeman, D.E. and Freeman, Y.S. (2001) *Between Worlds: Access to Second Language Acquisition* (2nd edn). Portsmouth, NH: Heinemann.

Genesee, F., Geva, E., Dressler, C. and Kamil, M. (2006) Synthesis: Cross-linguistic relationships. In D. August and T. Shanahan (eds) *Developing Literacy in Second-Language Learners: Report of the National Literacy Panel on Language-Minority Children and Youth* (pp. 153–174). Mahwah, NJ: Lawrence Erlbaum.

González-Howard, M. and McNeill, K.L. (2016) Learning in a community of practice: Factors impacting English-learning students' engagement in scientific argumentation. *Journal of Research in Science Teaching* 53 (4), 527–533.

Greene, J. (1999) A meta-analysis of the Rossell and Baker review of bilingual education research. *Bilingual Research Journal* 21 (2,3), 103–122.

Herrell, A.L. and Jordan, M. (2012) *50 Strategies for Teaching English Language Learners* (4th edn). Boston, MA: Pearson.

McField, G.P. and McField, D.R. (2014) The consistent outcome of bilingual education programs: A meta-analysis of meta-analyses. In G.P. McField (ed.) *The Miseducation of English Learners: A Tale of Three States and Lessons to be Learned* (pp. 267–298). Charlotte, NC: Information Age Publishing.

Ortega, L. (2008) *Understanding Second Language Acquisition*. New York: Routledge.

Porter, W., Riley, R., Towne, L., Hightower, A.M., Lloyd, S.C., Sellers, K.L. and Swanson, C.B. (2012) *Preparing for Change: A National Perspective on Common Core State Standards Implementation Planning.* Seattle, WA/Bethesda, MD: Education First/EPE Research Center. See www.edweek.org/media/preparingforchange-17standards.pdf (accessed 6 March 2018).

Rolstad, K., Mahoney, K. and Glass, G. (2005) The big picture: A meta-analysis of program effectiveness research on English language learners. *Educational Policy* 19 (4), 572–594.

Romaine, S. (1995) *Bilingualism* (2nd edn). Malden, MA: Blackwell Publishers.

Ryu, S. and Sandoval, W.A. (2012) Improvements to elementary children's epistemic understanding from sustained argumentation. *Science Education* 96 (3), 488–526.

Samson, J.F. and Collins, B.A. (2012) Preparing All Teachers to Meet the Needs of English Language Learners: Applying Research to Policy and Practice for Teacher Effectiveness. Washington, DC: Center for American Progress. See http://files.eric.ed.gov/fulltext/ED535608.pdf (accessed 6 March 2018).

Schleppegrell, M.J. (2004) *The Language of Schooling: A Functional Linguistics Perspective.* Mahwah, NJ: Lawrence Erlbaum.

Sutcher, L., Darling-Hammond, L. and Carver-Thomas, D. (2016) *A Coming Crisis in Teaching? Teacher Supply, Demand, and Shortages in the U.S.* Palo Alto, CA: Learning Policy Institute.

Thomas, W.P. and Collier, V.P. (2002) *A National Study of School Effectiveness for Language Minority Students' Long-Term Academic Achievement.* Santa Cruz, CA: University of California at Santa Cruz, Center for Research on Education, Diversity, and Excellence.

Wright, W.E. (2015) *Foundations for Teaching English Language Learners: Research, Theory, Policy, and Practice* (2nd edn). Philadelphia, PA: Caslon Publishing.

Zwiers, J. (2014) *Building Academic Language: Meeting Common Core Standards across Disciplines, Grades 5–12* (2nd edn). San Francisco, CA: Jossey-Bass.

5 "Languagizing" the Early Childhood Classroom: Supporting Children's Language Development

Rebecca M. Alper, Lillian R. Masek, Kathy Hirsh-Pasek, and Roberta Golinkoff

Research has shown that early language is the strongest predictor of children's school readiness and academic success in reading and writing (e.g., Dickinson *et al.*, 2003; Hoff, 2013; Neuman & Celano, 2006; NICHD, 2005; Pace *et al.*, in preparation; Snow *et al.*, 2007). A re-analysis of the NICHD Study of Early Child Care and Youth Development found that oral language in kindergarten predicted math and literacy performance in kindergarten, third, and fifth grade better than math, social, and reading scores. Moreover, oral language ability predicted *gains* in literacy and math from first to third and third to fifth grade (Burchinal *et al.*, 2016)! The quality and quantity of the language input that children receive in and out of school vary widely both across and within socioeconomic strata (Cartmill *et al.*, 2013; Hart & Risley, 1995; Hirsh-Pasek *et al.*, 2015), however, and many children are not exposed to language environments that support strong language learning before they enter school. Parents' knowledge of child development (Rowe, 2008), children's English language learner status (Hammer *et al.*, 2014), and their disability status (Paul & Elwood, 1991; Vigil *et al.*, 2005) can contribute to the level of language competence that children bring to school.

High-quality early childhood education (ECE) contributes to children's language skills (Justice *et al.*, 2008; Landry *et al.*, 2009; Vernon-Feagans & Bratsch-Hines, 2013; Wasik & Hindman, 2011), with teachers acting as the drivers of children's language development and thus their potential school success (Howes *et al.*, 2008). Although there has been little direct research on language interactions and outcomes in ECE classrooms (Neuman & Dwyer, 2009), the limited existing data show that high-quality classroom language environments are rare. Dickinson *et al.* (2014), for example, report that only 19% of language in ECE classrooms is high quality—characterized by diverse vocabulary, conceptual information about words, and sophisticated grammatical constructions. Furthermore, Marulis and Neuman (2010) suggest that while vocabulary interventions for preschoolers and kindergarteners are generally effective, children from low-income households tend to benefit less from these interventions than do their higher-income peers. In this chapter, we detail how early childhood teachers can optimize language input by *languagizing* their classrooms—establishing a culture of language and communication-rich interactions—to support all children, especially those with limited language and literacy input outside the classroom. Following Fillmore and Snow's (this volume) lead, we suggest that *languagizing* the classroom requires teachers to know a lot about language and use what they know to encourage conversation and enrich children's knowledge of words and grammar.

Children At Risk for Poorer Language and Academic Outcomes

Data from research on language development reveal that children in low-income households on average hear fewer and less diverse words, shorter and simpler sentences, more behavioral directives (e.g., "Come here"), fewer questions (e.g., "What is that?"), and fewer affirmations (e.g., "That's right!") than their higher-income peers (Aram *et al.*, 2013; Hart & Risley, 1995; Hoff, 2003; Huttenlocher *et al.*, 2010; Rowe, 2012). Children in poverty are less likely to experience sensitive, responsive, and cognitively stimulating interactions with caregivers, which support language growth (Bornstein *et al.*, 2008; Hirsh-Pasek *et al.*, 2015; Raviv *et al.*, 2004). These discrepancies in the quality and quantity of language input result in poorer language skills for children in poverty (Hart & Risley, 1995). While many criticize Hart and Risley's (1995) small sample size and poor operational definition of socioeconomic status, their results have been replicated (Hoff, 2003). It is important to keep in mind that these findings speak to child development in the aggregate, and there is heterogeneity within socioeconomic groups. Some low-income families have high-quality conversation in the home and some middle-income families do not. Many factors (e.g., caregiver depression and neighborhood resources) interact to influence parent–child interaction and hence language outcomes.

Children's language development in a given language is also impacted by other factors like how much input they hear in that language (Hoff *et al.*, 2012). This chapter focuses on English language skills—due to their importance in U.S. schools—but English language learners have skills in other languages that should be considered. English language learners generally hear less English than their monolingual peers, because they are learning more than one language. However, they may hear a higher proportion of English at home when a parent is a native English speaker (Place & Hoff, 2011) or when their older siblings attend English language schools (Bridges & Hoff, 2014). Place and Hoff (2011) found that two-year-olds' English proficiency was better predicted by their parents' English proficiency than the amount of English they heard. Thus, the quality of caregiver–child interaction may matter more than the quantity of English heard (Hirsh-Pasek *et al.*, 2015). These findings demonstrate that language environments are variable but malleable. Languagizing school environments in ways that help everyone—including typically developing children, those with disabilities, and children receiving limited input in the language of instruction outside the classroom—might go a long way toward ameliorating language gaps that may exist at school entry.

How can teachers *languagize* classrooms to optimize early language outcomes? Early caregiver–child communication data provide guidance. Here, we use that vast literature to present six evidence-based principles of language learning that suggest what ECE teachers need to know about language. Then we give examples of how to apply these principles in everyday classroom interaction.

Languagizing Classrooms: Six Principles

Findings from the language development literature can be distilled into six *languagizing* principles that are easy to understand and apply in the classroom (Table 5.1) (Konishi *et al.*, 2014: 406). *Languagizing* the classroom works when teachers apply these principles across all activities regardless of the content or focus (e.g., early numeracy, pre-literacy, and socio-emotional development [Kagan, *et al.*, 1995]).

Table 5.1 Six principles of language development

(1)	Children learn what they hear most.
(2)	Children learn words for things and events that interest them.
(3)	Interactive and responsive contexts rather than passive contexts promote language learning.
(4)	Children learn words best in meaningful contexts.
(5)	Children need to hear diverse examples of words and language structures.
(6)	Vocabulary and grammatical development are reciprocal processes.

From Principles to the Classroom

Children learn what they hear most

Preschool-aged children are characterized as emerging or developing language learners—given high-quality input, they rapidly expand their knowledge and production of speech sounds, vocabulary, grammar, and conversational skills. Children benefit from frequent exposure to words (Perry *et al.*, 2010) whether it is from repeated readings of a book or from conversation with an adult (McLeod & McDade, 2011). For example, when teachers read books about a *knight* who *vanquishes* a *dragon*, they can introduce new vocabulary about *castles, crenellations, moats*, and *shields*. Complementing the first book about knights and dragons with another one on a similar topic, or talking about the book beyond circle time helps children learn words while infusing them with meaning.

Children learn words for things and events that interest them

Interest breeds attention and increased attention leads to learning. When children become fascinated with dragons and the Knights of the Round Table, teachers can capitalize on this interest to emphasize the rich vocabulary tied to the theme of the Middle Ages. Through playful learning, the class can discover why moats were protective and why castles had high walls. Importantly, new vocabulary items associated with the theme do not emerge *de novo* when children are playing alone; they come from carefully crafted play environments that elicit play and conversation with adults who nest the new vocabulary in the child-initiated play scenes (Han *et al.*, 2010; Weisberg *et al.*, 2013).

Interactive and responsive rather than passive contexts promote language learning

To support language development, the learning environment must be both interesting and social. When teachers' talk is responsive and builds on children's interests, it supports language and literacy development (Hamre *et al.*, 2014). Volumes of data speak to the importance of conversation that goes beyond one turn—that builds beyond one right answer. The following exchange answers the question, but halts the conversation: CHILD: "What is this?" ADULT: "A moat." An alternative response from the adult continues the conversation for another turn: CHILD: "What is this?" ADULT: "That's called a moat. What do you think it does?" This conversational duet supports language growth (Goldin-Meadow *et al.*, 2014; Hirsh-Pasek *et al.*, 2015), and it requires more than one singer. The richness, responsivity, and continuity of teacher–child interactions matters.

Children learn words best in meaningful context

Throughout early childhood, children expand the range of functions for which they use language, like describing, requesting, asking and answering questions, telling stories, describing feelings, and discussing logical relationships (Pence & Justice, 2008). Children tend to learn language best in real-world situations as opposed to drill, and they benefit from learning related words together (Gelman & O'Reilly, 1988; Medin *et al.*, 2000; Rehder & Hastie, 2004). For instance, a conversation about how to build a castle can provide context for new words like *carpenter, mason, quarry, leverage*, and *hoist*. Contextualized interactions allow for the discussion of natural consequences and support language learning.

Children need to hear diverse examples of words and language structures

Frequent exposure to words is not enough to foster deep knowledge. Children learn new vocabulary best when they are shown multiple, diverse exemplars (e.g., real and imaginary castles, castles in different parts of the world [Rost, 2011]) and receive information about function (e.g., a castle was a home and a place of government) and conceptual relationships (e.g., a castle might have a *moat, tower, drawbridge*, and/or *turret*) as opposed to simply its shape or origin (Booth, 2009; Nelson *et al.*, 2008). Ideally, this kind of learning involves not only rich conversations about these qualities but also opportunities to learn through experience, including sociodramatic play, art projects, and field trips that bring the words to life.

Vocabulary and grammatical development are reciprocal processes

Learning new words helps children learn about grammar and vice versa. Children as young as two years rely on grammatical information to learn about new words in sentences. For instance, if a child hears "This is a _____," he/she can understand that the new word is a noun, whereas if he/she hears "The drawbridge goes _____ the moat," he/she can learn that the new word is a preposition, based on the sentence structure (Fisher *et al.*, 2006). The relationship between vocabulary and grammar extends to narrative: Children's narrative production and comprehension benefit from hearing adults tell stories about past and present events that are embedded in rich discourse (Peterson *et al.*, 1999; Reese *et al.*, 2010).

Envisioning the *Languagized* Classroom

Languagizing a classroom means applying these principles throughout the school day. Snapshots of the school day help illuminate the possibilities.

Arrival and greeting time

How can teachers *languagize* the moment when children arrive? Here is an opportunity for words of the day. Just as Groucho Marx had his descending duck when a contestant said the secret word, teachers can strike a bell whenever children use the day's word. The six principles provide a checklist for *languagizing* classroom activities like the morning routine. For example, in a classroom in San Francisco, the teacher fostered conversation by putting an everyday object like a wok in front of the class and declaring, "This is not a wok! What is it?" The kids all shared creative contributions that got the conversation going and that generated interest,

"This is a sled," one child proclaimed while climbing inside, "A hat," suggested another.

Reading time

Books offer new words that can be used to develop or enrich a theme throughout the week. Pictures and illustrations provide context and support related dramatic play. The principles can stimulate teacher planning around interacting with books. Which key words should be the focus and how might they be infused into discussion repeatedly? For example, if *drawbridge* is a key word, the teacher can ask children how they might fix the drawbridge if it was stuck. To extend a conversation, children can be asked to guess what happens next or to solve a problem such as how knights might find a fire-breathing dragon. A checklist containing the principles can serve as a reminder of ways to keep the conversation going.

Snack time

The snack routine gives children ample opportunities for initiating conversations, answering questions, and learning vocabulary items in context. Assigning children snack duties such as passing out napkins, offering snack choices to classmates, or cleaning up can provide meaningful language exposure and use. To reinforce spatial and math language—a foundation for science, technology, engineering, and mathematics (STEM) development—the teacher might ask, "How many napkins do you need for that table, Olivia?" Then the teacher would count them out with the child: "One, two, three...." Or the teacher might say, "Let's put the blue chair next to the green chair. Who wants to sit on the green chair?" Clean-up time offers other opportunities for *languagizing* the classroom using the principles to start a conversation during this everyday routine.

Play centers

Children are exposed to a lot of language as they rotate through activities. Teachers can use children's interest to enhance the language of their play and engage them in conversations. At the blocks station, teachers can reinforce the vocabulary that children learned during reading time (TEACHER: "I'm going to build a tower where the royal family can live. The horses will live outside in the stable."). This station can also foster math vocabulary and concepts (TEACHER: "I think this one should go on the bottom because it's really wide [while gesturing to demonstrate]"). In the dramatic play space, children can dress up as kings, queens, knights, and court jesters (TEACHER: "What kind of hat would the jester wear? What kind of tricks can he do?"). At the puzzle station, where children work together on a big puzzle, they practice teamwork and spatial skills (TEACHER: "This one is too big; can you pass me a smaller piece"?). The opportunities for *languagizing* play are endless.

Conclusion

Early language skills are critical for success in school and beyond, but not all children receive the language and literacy input outside of school that they need for school success. Fortunately, high-quality language interactions and conversations with early childhood teachers can help support these children. Although language learning is a complex process, there are simple ways for teachers to maximize children's language exposure and learning in the classroom. *Languagizing* the classroom does not require any special materials or extra time, but rather consciousness of applying scientific principles of language learning to everyday opportunities. By providing frequent exposure to high-quality language and many opportunities to communicate on topics that schools value, teachers can help *all* children learn the language that they need to be school ready.

References

Aram, D., Fine, Y. and Ziv, M. (2013) Enhancing parent-child shared book reading interactions: Promoting references to the book's plot and socio-cognitive themes. *Early Childhood Research Quarterly* 28 (1), 111–122.

Booth, A.E. (2009) Causal supports for early word learning. *Child Development* 80 (4), 1243–1250.

Bornstein, M.H., Tamis-LeMonda, C.S., Hahn, C.S. and Haynes, O.M. (2008) Maternal responsiveness to young children at three ages: Longitudinal analysis of a multidimensional, modular, and specific parenting construct. *Developmental Psychology* 44 (3), 867–874.

Bridges, K. and Hoff, E. (2014) Older sibling influences on the language environment and language development of toddlers in bilingual homes. *Journal of Applied Psycholinguistics* 35, 225–241.

Burchinal, M.R., Pace, A., Alper, R., Hirsh-Pasek, K. and Golinkoff, R.M. (July 2016) Early language outshines other predictors of academic and social trajectories in elementary school. Paper presented at the Association for Children and Families Conference (ACF), Washington, DC.

Cartmill, E.A., Armstrong, B.F., Gleitman, L.R., Goldin-Meadow, S., Medina, T.N. and Trueswell, J.C. (2013) Quality of early parent input predicts child vocabulary 3 years later. *Proceedings of the National Academy of Sciences of the United States of America* 110 (28), 11278–11283.

Dickinson, D.K., McCabe, A., Anastasopolous, L., Peisner-Feinberg, E.S. and Poe, M.D. (2003) The comprehensive language approach to early literacy: The interrelationships among vocabulary, phonological sensitivity, and print knowledge among preschool-aged children. *Journal of Educational Psychology* 95 (3), 465–481.

Dickinson, D.K., Hofer, K.G., Barnes, E.M. and Grifenhagen, J.F. (2014) Examining teachers' language in Head Start classrooms from a systemic linguistics approach. *Early Childhood Research Quarterly* 29 (3), 231–244.

Fisher, C., Klingler, S.L. and Song, H.J. (2006) What does syntax say about space? 2-year-olds use sentence structure to learn new prepositions. *Cognition* 101 (1), B19–B29.

Gelman, S.A. and O'Reilly, A.W. (1988) Children's inductive inferences within superordinate categories: The role of language and category structure. *Child Development* 59 (4), 876–887.

Goldin-Meadow, S., Levine, S.C., Hedges, L.V., Huttenlocher, J., Raudenbush, S.W. and Small, S.L. (2014) New evidence about language and cognitive development based on a longitudinal study: Hypotheses for intervention. *American Psychologist* 69 (6), 588–599.

Hammer, C.S., Hoff, E., Uchikoshi, Y., Gillanders, C., Castro, D.C. and Sandilos, L.E. (2014) The language and literacy development of young dual language learners: A critical review. *Early Childhood Research Quarterly* 29 (4), 715–733.

Hamre, B., Hatfield, B., Pianta, R. and Jamil, F. (2014) Evidence for general and domain-specific elements of teacher–child interactions: Associations with preschool children's development. *Child Development* 85 (3), 1257–1274.

Han, M., Moore, N., Vukelich, C. and Buell, M. (2010) Does play make a difference? How play intervention affects the vocabulary learning of at-risk preschoolers. *American Journal of Play* 3 (1), 82–105.

Hart, B. and Risley, T. (1995) *Meaningful Differences in the Everyday Experience of Young American Children*. Baltimore, MD: Brookes.

Hirsh-Pasek, K., Adamson, L.B., Bakeman, R., Owen, M.T., Golinkoff, R.M., Pace, A., Yust, P.K. and Suma, K. (2015) The contribution of early communication quality to low-income children's language success. *Psychological Science* 27 (7), 1071–1083.

Hoff, E. (2003) The specificity of environmental influence: Socioeconomic status affects early vocabulary development via maternal speech. *Child Development* 74 (5), 1368–1378.

Hoff, E. (2013) Interpreting the early language trajectories of children from low-SES and language minority homes: Implications for closing achievement gaps. *Developmental Psychology* 49 (1), 4–14.

Hoff, E., Core, C., Place, S., Rumiche, R., Señor, M. and Parra, M. (2012) Dual language exposure and early bilingual development. *Journal of Child Language* 39 (01), 1–27.

Howes, C., Burchinal, M., Pianta, R., Bryant, D., Early, D., Clifford, R. and Barbarin, O. (2008) Ready to learn? Children's pre-academic achievement in pre-kindergarten programs. *Early Childhood Research Quarterly* 23 (1), 27–50.

Huttenlocher, J., Waterfall, H., Vasilyeva, M., Vevea, J. and Hedges, L.V. (2010) Sources of variability in children's language growth. *Cognitive Psychology* 61 (4), 343–365.

Justice, L.M., Mashburn, A., Pence, K.L. and Wiggins, A. (2008) Experimental evaluation of a preschool language curriculum: Influence on children's expressive language skills. *Journal of Speech, Language, and Hearing Research* 51 (4), 983–1001.

Kagan, S.L., Moore, E. and Bradekamp, S. (eds) (1995) *Reconsidering Children's Early Learning and Development: Toward Common Views and Vocabulary (Report of the National Education Goals Panel, Goal 1 Technical Planning Group, No. ED 391 576)*. Washington, DC: U.S. Government Printing Office.

Konishi, H., Kanero, J., Freeman, M.R., Golinkoff, R.M. and Hirsh-Pasek, K. (2014) Six principles of language development: Implications for second language learners. *Developmental Neuropsychology* 39 (5), 404–420.

Landry, S.H., Anthony, J.L., Swank, P.R. and Monseque-Bailey, P. (2009) Effectiveness of comprehensive professional development for teachers of at-risk preschoolers. *Journal of Educational Psychology* 101 (2), 448–465.

Marulis, L.M. and Neuman, S.B. (2010) The effects of vocabulary intervention on young children's word learning: A meta-analysis. *Review of Educational Research* 80 (3), 300–335.

McLeod, A.N. and McDade, H.L. (2011) Preschoolers' incidental learning of novel words during storybook reading. *Communication Disorders Quarterly* 32 (4), 256–266.

Medin, D.L., Lynch, E.B. and Solomon, K.O. (2000) Are there kinds of concepts? *Annual Review of Psychology* 51, 121–147.

Nelson, D.G.K., O'Neil, K.A. and Asher, Y.M. (2008) A mutually facilitative relationship between learning names and learning concepts in preschool children: The case of artifacts. *Journal of Cognition and Development* 9 (2), 171–193.

Neuman, S.B. and Celano, D. (2006) The knowledge gap: Implications of leveling the playing field for low-income and middle-income children. *Reading Research Quarterly* 41 (2), 176–201.

Neuman, S.B. and Dwyer, J. (2009) Missing in action: Vocabulary instruction in pre-K. *The Reading Teacher* 62 (5), 384–392.

NICHD Early Child Care Research Network (2005) Pathways to reading: The role of oral language in the transition to reading. *Developmental Psychology* 41 (2), 428–442.

Pace, A., Alper, R., Burchinal, M., Golinkoff, R. and Hirsh-Pasek (2018). Measuring success: Within and cross-domain predictors of academic and social trajectories in elementary school. Manuscript submitted for publication.

Paul, R. and Elwood, T.J. (1991) Maternal linguistic input to toddlers with slow expressive language development. *Journal of Speech, Language, and Hearing Research* 34 (5), 982–988.

Pence, K.L. and Justice, L.M. (2008) *Language Development from Theory to Practice*. Upper Saddle River, NJ: Pearson Education, Inc.

Perry, L.K., Samuelson, L.K., Malloy, L.M. and Schiffer, R.N. (2010) Learn locally, think globally. Exemplar variability supports higher-order generalization and word learning. *Psychological Science* 21 (12), 1894–1902.

Peterson, C., Jesso, B. and McCabe, A. (1999) Encouraging narratives in preschoolers: An intervention study. *Journal of Child Language* 26 (01), 49–67.

Place, S. and Hoff, E. (2011) Properties of dual language exposure that influence 2-year-olds' bilingual proficiency. *Child Development* 82 (6), 1834–1849.

Raviv, T., Kessenich, M. and Morrison, F.J. (2004) A mediational model of the association between socioeconomic status and three-year-old language abilities: The role of parenting factors. *Early Childhood Research Quarterly* 19 (4), 528–547.

Reese, E., Leyva, D., Sparks, A. and Grolnick, W. (2010) Maternal elaborative reminiscing increases low-income children's narrative skills relative to dialogic reading. *Early Education and Development* 21 (3), 318–342.

Rehder, B. and Hastie, R. (2004) Category coherence and category-based property induction. *Cognition* 91 (2), 113–153.

Rost, G.C. (2011) Object categories provide semantic representation for 3-year-olds' word learning. Doctoral thesis, University of Iowa.

Rowe, M.L. (2008) Child-directed speech: Relation to socioeconomic status, knowledge of child development and child vocabulary skill. *Journal of Child Language* 35 (1), 185–205.

Rowe, M.L. (2012) A longitudinal investigation of the role of quantity and quality of child-directed speech in vocabulary development. *Child Development* 83 (5), 1762–1774.

Snow, C.E., Porche, M.V., Tabors, P.O. and Harris, S.R. (2007) *Is Literacy Enough? Pathways to Academic Success for Adolescents*. Baltimore, MD: Brookes.

Vernon-Feagans, L., Bratsch-Hines, M.E. and Family Life Project Key Investigators (2013) Caregiver-child verbal interactions in child care: A buffer against poor language outcomes when maternal language input is less. *Early Childhood Research Quarterly* 28 (4), 858–873.

Vigil, D.C., Hodges, J. and Klee, T. (2005) Quantity and quality of parental language input to late-talking toddlers during play. *Child Language Teaching and Therapy* 21 (2), 107–122.

Wasik, B.A. and Hindman, A.H. (2011) Improving vocabulary and pre-literacy skills of at-risk preschoolers through teacher professional development. *Journal of Educational Psychology* 103 (2), 455–469.

Weisberg, D.S., Hirsh-Pasek, K. and Golinkoff, R.M. (2013) Guided play: Where curricular goals meet a playful pedagogy. *Mind, Brain, and Education* 7 (2), 104–112.

6 Working with Families of Diverse Backgrounds: Learning from Teachers Who "Read" Their Students

Sonia Nieto

Changing student demographics in race, ethnicity, language, immigrant status, special needs, and other differences places a greater responsibility than ever on teachers to learn more about their students and how best to teach them. This situation is true for all teachers, but for teachers of English learners, it can be especially challenging. Nevertheless, as Fillmore and Snow remind us, every child in a U.S. classroom is an English learner whether they speak English as a native language or not. This means that teachers who learn how best to teach students learning English will be at an advantage in teaching all students.

Educators of English learners will find Chapter 1 by Fillmore and Snow very useful in terms of what they need to know about language. It is not only knowledge about language, however, with which teachers need to become familiar. Teachers also need to develop the dispositions that will help them be successful in teaching a diverse population, often the most complicated task of all.

Learning about their students' educational experiences as well as their families' cultures, histories, values, practices, and "funds of knowledge" (Moll *et al.*, 1992) is also crucial. But, first, a caution about "culture": While understanding the nature of culture is vital, the term itself has become so ubiquitous as to be meaningless and even harmful. Sometimes, culture is conflated with race, social class, or both; at other times, it is used to mean ethnicity or national origin; and worst of all, "culture" is too often viewed as a rigid collection of stereotypical behaviors, practices, and beliefs that define an entire group of people (Gorski, 2016; Nieto, 2010). For example, it is not uncommon to hear claims that particular families "don't care about education because it isn't part of their culture" (see, for example, the critique by Ladson-Billings, 2006). Instead, as Gutierrez and Rogoff (2003) have suggested, it is far more reasonable to use a cultural-historical perspective that recognizes culture as *practices* rather than characteristics since characteristics often get interpreted as fixed sets of behaviors and values. Culture is fluid and created by human beings, not a set of traits that we inherit through our DNA (for a fuller discussion of these issues, see chapter 3 in Nieto, 2010).

Profiles of Three Teachers

I have been privileged to work with many excellent teachers over my career as a teacher educator, including serving as their professor and mentor, engaging them in inquiry or reading groups, conducting research with them, or inviting them to contribute essays to some of my books. Some have been English as a second language (ESL) or bilingual teachers; others have worked primarily with students who speak a nonstandard version of English; and some have worked with what is generally considered a "mainstream" population of U.S. students, that is, middle-class, monolingual speakers of Standard English. Regardless of whom they teach, they have worked steadfastly to learn about their students, to provide them with equitable and socially just educational experiences, to form close and nurturing relationships with them, and to develop respectful partnerships with their families. Their experiences and insights are pertinent for all teachers regardless of the demographics of the students they teach. This chapter, then, is intended primarily for teachers of English learners, but it should be useful as well for all teachers because all classrooms are culturally diverse spaces, whether they appear to be or not.

In what follows, I address the following questions:

- Who are the students in our classrooms? What do teachers need to know about their histories, cultural traditions, practices, and values, and about their educational experiences?
- How can teachers learn about their students without falling into fixed generalizations and damaging stereotypes?
- What do teachers need to know about their students' families?
- What are the most productive ways of connecting with students' families?

I address these questions by presenting brief profiles of three teachers who exemplify the attitudes, behaviors, pedagogical strategies, and outreach approaches to families of diverse backgrounds that can serve as models for other teachers.

Learning who their students are means thinking about specific students, not some generic and generalized version of students, that is, not just that "Latin@ students like to work together," or that "Vietnamese students prefer learning on their own," as if these things held true for all students of particular backgrounds. For teachers of English learners, really learning about their students means addressing questions such as: What are their families' hopes and dreams for their children? What brought them here? Was it war, famine, personal family issues, or the desire to provide their children with better opportunities? And how can I reach out and learn from them?

Mary Cowhey: Who are the students?

Mary Cowhey, an award-winning elementary teacher in Massachusetts, got her start as a community organizer, a life that can only be described as one of commitment, hard work, and relentless struggle. It also prepared her with a great deal of knowledge and insights about diversity, culture, and social justice. Along the way, she learned to speak Spanish. But after 14 years as a community organizer, Mary decided it was time to do something more hopeful with her life, something that would give her more joy than the constant struggle and disappointment associated with community organizing. Teaching seemed like the perfect option.

Mary described why she became a teacher by saying, "[B]eing a multicultural educator is my contribution to world peace and a more just and peaceful community" (Gebhard et al., 2002: 234). She returned to college to earn her bachelor's degree and, after graduating, immediately applied to the graduate program in bilingual, ESL, and multicultural education at the University of Massachusetts–Amherst where I became her mentor. From the start, Mary has had a special commitment to English learners and always wanted to work proactively with families. Starting in her first year of teaching, she asked that all the English learners of the grade she taught be clustered in her classroom.

Mary has shared inspiring examples of her teaching (e.g., Cowhey, 2006). Though well versed in linguistic, literacy, and cultural insights, she has never assumed that she knew enough about her particular students to know what they and their families wanted for them. She made it a point to get to know her students before the beginning of the school year. Referring to Paulo Freire's (1998) admonition that before teaching students to read, teachers need to "read the students," Mary wrote about how she does this, explaining her reasoning:

> You write about reading the class. I guess I jump the gun.... I spend the week before the first day of school visiting my students' homes, meeting the students and their families.... That way I know where my students are coming from, literally. I know who their people are. I know the names their families call them. I know what they are proud of and what worries them. I begin to trust these families. My students and their families begin to trust me. (Cowhey, 2008: 13)

Mary shared a particularly powerful example of this practice when she wrote about visiting one of her students' families in the homeless shelter where they were living. It says a lot about the tremendous respect she had already garnered in the community that not only was she invited to the homeless shelter, but also she was in fact warmly welcomed into that space.

In her first years in the classroom, Mary found that English learners were often silenced, inadvertently or not, by other students. In her first year of teaching, she had a native English speaker whom she described as always "jumping in and cutting other students off" (Gebhard *et al.*, 2002: 236). In the same class, a Puerto Rican English learner would raise her hand to respond but she needed time to get her thoughts together. The other students noticed how unfair it was that this girl was frequently cut off before she could answer. After speaking about this with the class, Mary explained, "The kids generated this rule that 'you can't step on someone else's words' because it messes up what they are trying to say" (Gebhard *et al.*, 2002: 236), one of the best examples I've seen of working proactively with students to help them understand language issues.

Mary recently wrote, "I've been a teacher for 17 years and a community organizer for 35 years" (Cowhey, 2016: 190). For her, teaching *is* organizing. For example, along with a colleague and some parents, several years ago Mary started Families with Power/*Familias con Poder*, a community organization of low-income families dedicated to promoting grassroots leadership among parents and youth. The group began by meeting in the living rooms of participating families, reading with children. In the process, not only have children improved their literacy, but also parents and other family members have been mobilized and empowered.

After a dozen years teaching first and second grade, Mary took on a new challenge, becoming a Title 1 math teacher and coach of children from kindergarten to third grade. Regardless of the subject matter, Mary's commitment to her students and their families has never waned. She continues to "read" them in order to be able to teach them, not just reading, science, and social justice, but now primarily math. When she was asked to take on this position, she requested that it include a family engagement component. Given her success with family outreach over the years, her principal readily agreed. Families with Power/*Familias con Poder* has evolved to feature activities in the school itself including Morning Math Club, described as an organization "staffed by parents who were all English language learners, most of whom had not graduated from high school" (Cowhey, 2016: 191). In its third year, the club meets twice a week before school with an average of 25 K–4 students and 7 parents "to have fun learning and playing with math together, while affirming their families' funds of knowledge and cultivating leadership" (Cowhey, 2016: 192). In her essay, Mary explained that for her, teaching mathematics, like teaching anything else, means promoting social justice and equity (Cowhey, 2016).

Angeles Pérez: Nurturing relationships

Aside from learning the content they need to teach and the pedagogical strategies to teach it, the most important job for teachers is to form relationships of caring and respect with their students (Noddings, 1992; Valenzuela, 1999). This should go without saying, of course, but it isn't always clear in the scarce attention that colleges of education and school-based professional development pay to this issue. Instead, many professional development activities focus almost entirely on methods without acknowledging that methods alone do not guarantee that teachers will be able to connect with their students.

Creating time to relate to students is one way to create nurturing relationships. Angeles Pérez, who was a second-year bilingual fourth-grade teacher in Texas when I interviewed her a number of years ago (she is now an assistant principal), formed a caring learning community by building relationships with each of her students. She did this in numerous ways, both through the curriculum and outside of it. For example, she made it a point to reserve 10 minutes at the end of each day as "Hanging out with Ms. Pérez time." In this way, she learned something about each student's interests and experiences, information that she could later use in her curriculum and outreach with families. "Hanging out with Ms. Pérez time" gave students the opportunity to share what was on their minds, and to ask her any questions they had about her, her family, the school, or nearly anything else. They would also share their own dreams for the future, or concerns about their families. It was, in effect, a time to build authentic relationships.

With knowledge, a desire to work with students who deserve good teachers, and unstoppable energy, Angeles chose to begin her career in a predominantly Mexican American, high-poverty, low-resourced school. She did so purposefully because she knew that other teachers would choose an easier path, and yet, as she said during an interview, "What about the kids that it's not their fault? Because they're economically disadvantaged, they're going to get stuck with the leftovers?" (Nieto, 2013: 37). She bubbled over with enthusiasm when speaking about her students: "I'm their biggest fan!" she said (Nieto, 2013: 38).

Probably the most valuable attitude that Angeles has brought to the profession is a fierce rejection of the deficit thinking that characterizes so many urban schools attended by children living in poverty. This attitude was also evident in her relationships with families. It is all too common for educators working with marginalized students in high-poverty schools to bemoan the lack of participation of families in school events. Teachers may sometimes conclude that parents just don't care. Yet, too often, teachers know little about the families of their students, about what brought them to this country, or about their history and experiences. Families, in turn, may be unfamiliar with the school's expectations—particularly if expectations in their home countries were far different—or they may feel uncomfortable or unwelcome in the school. Parents may not speak English or they may be working or need to care for other children or family members.

Angeles, however, believed that all parents are interested in, and committed to, their children's education. She regularly communicated with them and was successful in getting several parents to volunteer in her classroom. What was most important, she said, was to personalize communication with them. She didn't just call them when children misbehaved, but instead reached out with good news or questions or invitations to events. She gave the example of a "Dad's Night" the school sponsored. "We had a Dad's Night; three hundred dads showed up! That was amazing and it was because all week I was building it up with any student I saw in the hallway. We had so many dads we didn't know what to do!" (Nieto, 2013: 45).

Little things mean a lot when teachers relate to their students in authentic ways. Even as a first-year teacher, Angeles wanted to show her students and their families that she cared about them and expected the best from them. For instance, she started and ended each day by expressing her happiness in having her students in her classroom. She said,

> I make it a point to greet them at the door every day. I'm at the door, I'm smiling. And at the end of each day, they run to give me a hug and it's the best feeling because they care so much about me. They will work for me because they know I work for them. I love them. (Nieto, 2013: 38)

Another strategy that Angeles developed in her first year of teaching was to help each student set his/her own learning goals. She then worked with each student individually to help them reach those goals, making revisions when necessary. She explained, "I pride myself on getting them to set their goals and they're not low goals, they're high goals" (Nieto, 2013: 39). Angeles said that high test scores, meeting the federal Annual Yearly Progress requirement, and other mandates were not what drove her; instead, it was her students' excitement about learning. She assumed they would do well on tests because she was teaching them well. In fact, even the students she taught her first year did extremely well on the high-stakes state test, something that surprised her colleagues and administrators. But for Angeles, this happened primarily because of the relationship she had with her students. She mentioned one student who, at the beginning of the year, was classified as a nonreader; he was convinced he wouldn't make it to fifth grade. "He's reading fifth-grade books now," she said proudly (Nieto, 2013: 40).

Angeles described a day that was particularly significant for her: It was when one of her students won the Spelling Bee. Though this may not seem particularly groundbreaking, it was highly unusual for two reasons: first, because she taught fourth grade in a K–5 school and usually it was a fifth grader who won; but even more significant, because it was the first time a Latino Spanish-dominant student from a bilingual class had won this contest. Angeles was so excited that she ran down the hall shouting, "… my student just won the Spelling Bee! I can't believe it!" She added, "That for me is so big that I feel like *I* won the spelling bee! Their success is my success, I guess" (Nieto, 2013: 38).

Carmen Tisdale: Speaking their words and dreaming big

Giving children the opportunity to envision new possibilities, teachers become social and cultural mediators for their students. Carmen Tisdale demonstrates this in her second-grade classroom every day. A teacher for 16 years, the past 8 or so in a predominantly Black elementary school in Columbia, South Carolina, Carmen is a National Board Certified teacher and former finalist for Teacher of the Year in her district. She has been active in the National Council of Teachers of English and its Early Childhood Education Assembly.

Being African American herself, Carmen believes she has a responsibility to be a role model, encouraging her students to dream big. She spoke, for example, about Jamal, who said he wanted to be a bus driver when he grew up. During our interview, Carmen said:

> So I'm always the one to say, "I want you to think about owning a fleet of buses." There's nothing wrong with being a bus driver, there's nothing wrong with being anything that you are if that's what you truly want to be and you're good at it, but I feel he's saying that because that's what he knows and he rides the bus every morning. (Nieto, 2013: 54)

In spite of the limited possibilities they may see around them, Carmen constantly reminds her students of their value and their potential. This is not so much a strategy as it is a mindset, one that would be useful for any teacher to adopt. During our interview, Carmen said:

> I think to be a good teacher you need to love your children in spite of themselves, in spite of whatever they bring to you. You love them unconditionally and you tell them that you love them. (Nieto, 2013: 49)

Carmen believes that children need to see their culture and race reflected in the people around them, including teachers. As a result, she brings her entire self into the classroom. She spoke about being a "Black Momma" because it connects culturally with her students and is a powerful way to communicate that she cares about them. Being a "Black Momma" is both a stance and a way of speaking. "We just have—and I'm sure all cultures do—a certain way to talking, there's a rhythm to it. We all bring our culture to the classroom whether we realize it or not" (Nieto, 2013: 54). She explained that just using African American English created a mutual understanding with her students. "I might say, 'Get your behind over there and sit down.' That's what your Black Momma would say, and it's not to say that every Black Momma would say it" (Nieto, 2013: 54). She went on to give another example:

> You know how it is, you're the social worker and advocate; you are the momma. "I'm putting shea butter on your little ashy face." That's what your momma does.... I really am a part of that village it takes to raise a kid. (Nieto, 2013: 55)

However, as I often remind teachers, not everyone can be a "Black Momma." Most of all, being culturally responsive means being authentic, true to one's own culture. But even teachers from backgrounds different from their students can be culturally responsive by demonstrating care and having high expectations for their students.

At the same time that Carmen uses African American English to connect with her students, she said it was important to maintain a balance between African American English and language that is socially acceptable in general society, in this case, Standard English. She explained:

> I know I have to teach them language that is accepted in school, but I also give them confirmation that their home language is a real language. There is nothing wrong with it. In some ways, I feel I offer them validation of who they are, and I understand them just because of who I am. They get to see themselves and experience the familiar while learning outside of their box. (Nieto, 2013: 55)

Another way in which Carmen uses students' identities is in her explicit curriculum. Her brother, a rapper, composed a rap about famous African Americans for her students. They were immediately engaged and learned not only a rap song but social studies and research skills:

> I stretched their learning and made them see their own possibilities as we did research projects and wrote letters to some of the people in the rap song. I was able to show them that these are real people who live real lives today. They could be one of these people. (Nieto, 2013: 55)

Conclusion

Mary Cowhey, Angeles Pérez, and Carmen Tisdale exemplify teachers who are adept at "reading" their students by affirming their identities and their languages, and by using students' cultural experiences, expressions, and practices in their curriculum and pedagogy. Most of all, they challenge ubiquitous deficit perspectives in schools and society, and they build on students' resources and families' funds of knowledge. In this chapter, we have seen them do these things in a variety of ways: They invite parents to volunteer in the classroom; they work with families before and after school; they challenge their own ideas and perspectives and those of others; they use culturally responsive teaching approaches; they do home visits; and they create special times to get to know their students. Most of all, they show their students that they love them.

Also evident in all of these examples is that teachers who are responsive to their students and their students' families define themselves first and foremost as learners. Teachers such as Mary Cowhey, Angeles Pérez, and Carmen Tisdale understand that effective teaching begins with learning about their students in order to build a climate of care in their classrooms. "Culture" becomes a creative endeavor rather than a fixed set of characteristics as teachers, students, and families work hard at developing relationships of learning and responsibility.

References

Cowhey, M. (2006) *Black Ants and Buddhists: Thinking Critically and Teaching Differently in the Primary Grades*. Portland, ME: Stenhouse.

Cowhey, M. (2008) Reading the class. In S. Nieto (ed.) *Dear Paulo: Letters from Those Who Dare Teach* (pp. 10–16). Boulder, CO: Paradigm.

Cowhey, M. (2016) Doing social justice work through math. In S. Nieto (ed.) *Why We Teach Now* (pp. 183–193). New York: Teachers College Press.

Freire, P. (1998) *Teachers as Cultural Workers: Letters to Those Who Dare Teach*. Boulder, CO: Westview Press.

Gebhard, M., Austin, T., Nieto, S. and Willett, J. (2002) "You can't step on someone else's words": Preparing all teachers to teach language minority students. In Z. Beykont (ed.) *The Power of Culture: Teaching across Language Difference* (pp. 219–243). Cambridge, MA: Harvard Educational Publishing Group.

Gorski, P. (2016) Rethinking the role of "culture" in educational equity: From cultural competence to equity literacy. *Multicultural Perspectives* 18 (4), 221–226.

Gutierrez, K. and Rogoff, B. (2003) Cultural ways of learning: Individual traits or repertoires of practice. *Education Researcher* 32 (5), 19–25.

Ladson-Billings, G. (2006) It's not the culture of poverty, it's the poverty of culture: The problem with teacher education. *Anthropology and Education Quarterly* 37 (2), 104–109.

Moll, L.C., Gonzalez, N., Amanti, C. and Neff, D. (1992) Funds of knowledge for teaching: A qualitative approach to connect households and classrooms. *Theory into Practice* 31 (2), 132–141.

Nieto, S. (2010) *The Light in Their Eyes: Creating Multicultural Learning Communities*. 10th anniversary edition. New York: Teachers College Press.

Nieto, S. (2013) *Finding Joy in Teaching Students of Diverse Backgrounds: Culturally Responsive and Socially Just Practices in U.S. Classrooms*. Portsmouth, NH: Heinemann Publishers.

Noddings, N. (1992) *The Challenge to Care in Schools: An Alternative Approach to Education*. New York: Teachers College Press.

Valenzuela, A. (1999) *Subtractive Schooling: U.S.-Mexican Youth and the Politics of Caring*. Albany, NY: State University of New York Press.

7 What Teachers Need to Know About Language: A Focus on Language Disorders

Li-Rong Lilly Cheng

This chapter takes a speech pathologist's perspective on providing guidance for teachers about how they may differentiate students who are becoming bilingual/multilingual in typical ways from those who are not. Because teachers in U.S. schools have daily encounters with students who are learning English, they play a critical role in recommending individual students for special services and helping them to learn successfully in their classrooms. Thus, it is extremely useful for them to have knowledge about language (as Fillmore & Snow [this volume] articulate), in particular language learning, in order to distinguish language and other disorders from predictable behaviors related to language learning.

Myth or Reality?

The English word *education* has two different Latin roots: *educare*, which means to train or to mold, and *educere*, which means to lead or draw out. How do teachers draw out the best from their students? How do they view students who do not know English and are struggling to be understood or heard? How do teachers react to silence or "no call, no show" from parents who simply do not know what the school is expecting? Teachers must not give up when it is difficult to lead students or communicate with parents.

A teacher brings to his/her classroom a set of values, beliefs, and biases. Biases are learned and can be reduced with effort (Cheng, 2009). Investigating the cultural, linguistic, institutional, psychological, social, familial, and personal factors that influence perceptions and biases is crucial to everyday life and social/cultural encounters in schools. We need to debunk myths based on racial or ethnic stereotypes and face the realities of multiplicities. To reduce our personal biases, we need to shift our theoretical paradigm from looking at bilingual/multicultural students as having challenges in school to looking at them as agents of change for our own mindset and as bringing language resources to our classrooms. As Fillmore and Snow (this volume) assert, knowledge about language learning and development can help teachers confront stereotypes and facilitate student learning. Some fundamental concepts that need to be examined include the process of learning two languages consecutively, the impact of acculturation within the context of the acquisition of a new language, and the many factors that influence school outcomes. As projected by Friedman (2005), the world is getting flatter, which means that we have an urgent need to understand more about peoples and cultures that we do not know. The approach discussed in this chapter may come in handy for professionals who work with children who are linguistically diverse and may not be neurotypical.

English learners come to our schools with diverse cultural and linguistic backgrounds and speak a variety of home languages. Their level of English language proficiency and their diverse backgrounds may result in behaviors that diverge from school expectations. Teachers of English learners may notice that students display some of the following characteristics, which may either be seen as red flags or considered common for new arrivals and beginning English language learners:

1. insufficient overall communication skills in English,
2. diverse linguistic and social knowledge and educational background,
3. varying degrees of home language literacy,
4. varying degrees of proficiency in English,
5. varying degrees of metalinguistic awareness,
6. a foreign accent in English,
7. limited English vocabulary development,
8. delay in knowledge gain,
9. difficulty in articulation,
10. apparent lack of interest in communication,
11. lack of attention during a joint activity (for example, reading a book together),
12. lack of gestures,
13. slow response time,
14. lack of nonverbal communication.

Language Difference or Disorder?

How can we tell a language difference from a language disorder? What are the red flags signaling possible disorders when an English learner enters school? Teachers may view an English learner's lack of progress in English as typical and attribute all unusual language behaviors to developing English language proficiency. In fact, there are some warning signs (red flags) that they should pay attention to. These characteristics could signal that lack of progress in language learning is caused by a neurological disorder or other types of language/communicative disorders. One important indicator of a language disorder appears when neither the student's parents nor siblings understand the student. Another important indicator appears when the student often plays alone. While this behavioral pattern may be explained by shyness or fear, it may also suggest a disorder. If teachers pay attention to playing behaviors among students, they may gain important clues to a possible communicative disorder.

When an English learner displays signs that deviate from typical bilingual acquisition patterns, there may be comments like the following: "Since the student is learning two languages, it will take longer for him or her to learn to speak, so even if the student is a bit delayed, the student will catch up" (Cheng, 2011). This stance is inaccurate, and it is a dangerous assumption because it can obscure real problems. Some fundamental principles can guide teachers in distinguishing language differences from disorders:

1. A child with a language disorder experiences difficulties in both the mother tongue and another language (including the school language). The problem lies in the ability to process linguistic signals rather than multiple language exposure.
2. A child with a language disorder can learn two or three languages. The issue of learning languages is not how many but how.
3. Languages are not learned in a vacuum: They are best learned in a language-rich environment.
4. Superficial and initial difficulties in learning the school language do not result in a language disorder later on.
5. A child with a language disorder secondary to developmental disorders such as autism spectrum disorder behaves similarly in different language environments whether bilingual, monolingual, or mixed.
6. Because foreign language-influenced accents can present a challenge for intelligibility, the child may be viewed as not intelligent, but accent is not necessarily related to intelligence.

Teachers who understand these principles will be better able to decide when to make a referral for evaluation.

The following sections offer some strategies that are recommended for teachers who need to investigate a student's language development or who suspect a language disorder, along with two student case studies of these strategies in use.

Strategies for Investigating Possible Language Disorders among English Learners

Wallach (2011) describes the process of getting to know a child and his/her language development as "peeling an onion." There are layers and layers of information, all of which must be taken into consideration when working with the child and the family. Cheng (2006) advocates using the RIOT (Review, Interview, Observe, and Test) approach in the assessment of a student's language competence and communicative competence. Teachers can use this approach to tease out red flags that could signal possible language disorders and to learn about normal behaviors for students who are learning English as a new language.

The RIOT approach involves the following:

1. Review: Review all pertinent data about the student: birth, early development, family background, language background, school records, medical records, and so forth. If there are no previous concerns about language learning, then the student may not be at risk.
2. Interview: Interview family members (parents and siblings) as well as other caretakers, teachers, former teachers, classmates, schoolmates, and so forth. Again, if no concerns are expressed by the family and others, then the student may be going through a transitional period rather than exhibiting signs of a disorder.
3. Observe: Observe the student interacting with parents, siblings, other family members, and classmates, in the classroom and around the school. Observations can reveal a lot of information about social, psychological, and learning behaviors.
4. Test: Conduct informal and formal tests including collecting language samples in different languages. Teachers can certainly get language samples in English to establish the baseline for English. Further testing by speech/language pathologists can be requested if there are red flags.

Using this approach, teachers can gather useful information about students to answer questions such as the following, probing for additional details as needed:

1. Do the student's parents understand her/him?
2. Do the student's siblings understand her/him?
3. Who does the student play with?
4. If the student has playmates, do they understand her/him?
5. Can anyone understand the student?
6. What does the student like to do?
7. What does the student like to play?
8. What does the student like to eat?
9. Who are the significant people in the student's environment?
10. What is a typical day for this student?

If they have used the RIOT approach to answer these kinds of background questions, teachers will be in a better position to provide pertinent information when they participate in an individual education plan meeting to discuss a student case with other school personnel, including a speech/language pathologist. The speech/language pathologist will typically prepare a speech and language assessment report for the meeting, containing the following types of information (Cheng, 1996, 1997):

1. diagnosis/reason for referral,
2. concerns expressed by parents with regard to their child's development,
3. medical history,
4. behavioral observation,
5. clinical observation,
6. results of tests conducted,

    a. receptive and expressive language skills,
    b. language comprehension,
    c. language expression,
    d. oral motor skills and articulation,
    e. pragmatic language,
    f. basic concepts,
    g. language sample and story retelling task.

Both the "peeling an onion" approach and the RIOT approach stress the importance of teachers who have an opportunity to observe student behavior over time and in different contexts. A holistic analysis like the RIOT procedure, which uses information from the case history and clinical analysis, is well suited to capture a clear profile of the child's communication skills (Cheng, 2007a) as part of the determination of whether or not a disorder may need to be treated.

The following case studies illustrate what peeling the onion and the RIOT approach contribute to understanding a student's atypical language behavior.

Case study: Shawn

Shawn, a sixth grader, was evaluated by a monolingual English-speaking speech/language pathologist. Her report (paraphrased here) indicated the following issues: Shawn sometimes demonstrated unusual social behavior, including on the one hand, avoiding human interaction and eye contact completely, or on the other hand, intruding on someone else's personal space with penetrating eye contact, doing what speech pathologists refer to as "soul tapping" (he has done this since he was a toddler). There is an extreme contrast in Shawn's ability to focus in an independent situation compared with that behavior in a group situation. His comfort level for communicating with others increases dramatically as he learns their speech patterns. Prior evaluation by an audiologist indicated that Shawn has central auditory processing disorder and suggested fitting earplugs and/or earmuffs for use during desk and study activities, and providing a custom-designed filter for his left ear.

The speech/language pathologist did not suggest testing in languages other than English. Shawn's mother was not satisfied with the speech/language pathologist's report and sought a consultation from a multilingual practitioner. The following is the initial result of that consultation based on the use of the peeling the onion and RIOT approaches.

R: Review of the case history. Shawn is a sixth-grade Italian student who has been referred for evaluation in a school district in the United States because of concerns about atypical language and other behaviors. He has lived in a number of countries and is now in the United States attending a public school. Very little information about his former schooling is available. His past experience includes living in Italy and elsewhere. His parents are Italian/English bilinguals. He attended international schools where English was the school language. He has been with caretakers who speak a variety of languages (Bahasa Indonesia, Ilocano, and Tamil) and marginal English. He presents to the school district with limited expressive English language skills, but his mother reported that he has many other language skills and that he learned Chinese online.

I: Interviews. Shawn's mother was interviewed extensively. She had been fighting a custody battle with her former husband, and with the intervention of the U.S. consulate she was finally able to gain full custody of Shawn. She indicated that Shawn was taken care of mostly by nannies who spoke minimal English and there was no supervision of homework at home. His father and later his stepmother were seldom home, leaving him to the care of the nannies. Shawn's mother thinks that her son is a gifted child and wanted him tested. His mother also indicated that he is language-locked and as a result, he is very socially inhibited. His talents are being masked by his communication difficulties. She thinks he has a gift for learning languages and music. He taught himself Chinese through online instruction. He was able to repeat sentences in Chinese with accurate tones, and he also learned how to write Chinese logographic characters.

The discussion revealed that Shawn's mother was not allowed to be with him or see him for more than five years, and she has no school records to review. Based on this interview, it was clear that a thorough and comprehensive evaluation is needed.

O: Observations. Shawn was observed by a speech pathologist in a setting where he interacted with his mother. For the most part, his mother did the talking, and Shawn seemed to understand simple sentences. Shawn was also observed working with a Chinese language teacher and he repeated phrases with 90% accuracy. When he was asked questions, he repeated the questions. When correct answers were provided, he also repeated the answers. He lacked eye contact but did follow the flow of the Chinese language lessons by turning the pages and looking at the pages, and he repeated after the teacher. He could identify some nouns by pointing to pictures correctly. He perseverated on certain words that he was interested in. A thorough assessment of Shawn in English, Italian, and Chinese is highly recommended.

T: **Testing.** Due to Shawn's linguistic-cultural background and behavioral concerns, several alternative testing methods were used to create a communication profile. These methods, some of which overlap with the Interview and Observe components of the RIOT approach, included assessment in other languages by a speech/language pathologist with interpreters (Langdon & Cheng, 2002; Langdon & Saenz, 2016), in-depth parent and teacher interviews, and comprehensive language samples.

From the evidence collected from these various sources, a potential diagnosis of autism spectrum disorder was suggested for Shawn. A referral for a thorough evaluation and an individual education plan was recommended.

Many teachers perceive students who are learning English as needing time to learn the language before referral, while monolingual students presenting evidence of disorders and syndromes such as autism spectrum disorders, attention deficit disorder, and other syndromes tend to be identified for referral early (Kennedy & Banks, 2016; Prizant, 2016). Teachers who work with a child on the autism spectrum who is bilingual/multilingual must be informed about how to peel the onion and not let superficial impressions based on the student's bilingual/multilingual background mask the true disorder, as illustrated by Shawn's situation.

Case study: Meimei

Meimei is a seven-year-old bilingual Chinese/English-speaking girl adopted by her American parents 20 months ago from northern China. She is currently repeating first grade and has great difficulty communicating. She can say some phrases in English but does not demonstrate understanding of simple questions (e.g., she could not respond when asked, "Where are you going?") in either Mandarin or English. Her language skills appeared to be delayed prior to the adoption, but she was reported to be able to speak four- to five-word simple sentences and understand simple directions in Chinese. She has not been exposed to her mother tongue (Mandarin) since she arrived in the United States. At this time, she almost seems not to know any Chinese. Her adoptive parents plan to adopt another child, a 10-year-old girl from China, and they hope that the older child can help Meimei with Chinese. They want Meimei to maintain her Mandarin language, but they were told by a professional speech/language pathologist to provide her with exposure to English only in order not to confuse her. A school parent who is a native Mandarin speaker indicated that when she talked to Meimei she found Meimei capable of understanding Chinese and able to use simple sentences.

Once again, peeling the onion and using the RIOT procedure can help the teacher to understand the student's situation. The teacher's interview provided information about Meimei's strengths:

1. She is friendly toward other classmates.
2. She attempts to participate in all activities.
3. She watches how other students do things in class and imitates them.

Weaknesses noted are as follows:

1. Meimei requires lots of support to communicate ideas.
2. She has limited vocabulary.
3. She speaks in short phrases.

More probing is needed to get a complete picture of this student. Taking the next steps, a teacher would make a referral for special needs evaluation, and a comprehensive Student Study Team would be established to complete the assessment process. Once a comprehensive assessment is done, a report (such as that described above) would be available for consideration in determining the best course for the student.

The Teacher's Crucial Role

There is a lot to learn about students who have been referred for speech and language assessment, and the teacher's role in gathering information is critical. Teachers need to know about the bilingual language competence of their students (Cheng, 1999, 2004, 2007a, 2007b; Grech & Dodd, 2007), which requires them to know a great deal about language and language development.

Teachers need to understand also that students present different kinds of Englishes. This fact needs to be recognized in language assessments and observations. Amy Tan, author of *The Joy Luck Club* (Tan, 1989), explains in an essay titled "Mother Tongue" (Tan, 2007) that she "began to write stories using all the Englishes [she] grew up with." For monolinguals, the different Englishes may mean the English used in schools or formal settings (formal English); the English used for everyday conversation (informal or casual English); the English used among close friends (intimate English); the English used among gang members (coded English); or the English used in cyberspace (cyber English). But for English learners, the situation is different. Tan (2007) described four types of Englishes that she experienced:

1. the "broken English" that her mother speaks,
2. the "water-down English" that Tan translates for her mother from Chinese,
3. the "simple English" that Tan uses with her mother,
4. English translated from her mother's Chinese that captures her communicative intent.

Understanding the process of learning English and the many forms of English that students and families have experienced, as well as the differences between language disorders and language differences, will assist teachers of English learners in providing optimal English language learning experiences for their students, as well as making appropriate referrals for speech/language assessment. Many schools offer bilingual and even trilingual programs, and success stories of these programs have been reported (Park, personal communication, 2016). In the event that a school does not provide bilingual speech and language services, teachers must be prepared to work with students to provide an optimal language learning environment and experience for the students (Cheng, 2011).

Conclusion

Differentiating students who are typically developing bilingual/multilingual individuals from those who are not requires thorough investigation. In achieving this purpose, all languages that the students know need to be assessed, and it should be recognized that an interpreter may be needed (Langdon & Cheng, 2002; Langdon & Saenz, 2016). Understanding the background of the students must be the foundation for this work (Cheng et al., 2014). Teachers who know about language play an important role in the process of identifying students learning English who have language disorders.

References

Cheng, L. (1996) Beyond bilingualism: A quest for communicative competence. *Topics in Language Disorders* 16 (4), 9–21.

Cheng, L. (1997) Asian and Pacific American cultures. In D. Battle (ed.) *Communication Disorders in Multicultural Populations* (pp. 73–116). Boston, MA: Butterworth-Heinemann.

Cheng, L. (1999) Moving beyond accent: Social and cultural realities of living with many tongues. *Topics in Language Disorders* 19 (4), 1–10.

Cheng, L. (2004) The challenge of hyphenated identity. *Topics in Language Disorders* 24 (3), 216–224.

Cheng, L. (2006, September 14–16) Lessons from the Da Vinci Code. *ASHA Leader Online*. See http://www.asha.org/about/publications/leader (accessed 1 March 2018).

Cheng, L. (2007a) Cultural intelligence (CQ): A quest for cultural competence. *Communication Disorders Quarterly* 29 (1), 36–42.

Cheng, L. (2007b) Codes and contexts: Exploring linguistic, cultural, and social intelligence. *ASHA Leader Online* 12 (7), 8–9, 32–33. See https://leader.pubs.asha.org/article. aspx?articleid=2278175 (accessed 1 March 2018).

Cheng, L. (2009) Creating an optimal language learning environment: A focus on family and culture. *Communication Disorders Quarterly* 30 (2), 69–76.

Cheng, L. (2011) Working with English language learners with special needs. Selected Proceedings of the 2011 Michigan Teachers of English to Speakers of Other Languages Conference, Kalamazoo, Michigan, October 7–8, 2011.

Cheng, L., Wallach, G. and Reed, V.A. (2014) ASHA SLPs in China teach teachers about their students with disabilities. *Communication Disorders Quarterly* 36 (2), 119–120.

Friedman, T.L. (2005) *The World Is Flat: A Brief History of the Twenty-First Century.* New York: Farrar, Straus and Giroux.

Grech, H. and Dodd, B. (2007) Assessment of speech and language skills in bilingual children: A holistic approach. *Stem, Sparaak en Tsalpathologie* 15 (2), 84–92.

Kennedy, D.M. and Banks, R.S. (2016) *Bright Not Broken: Gifted Kids, ADHD and Autism.* New York: John Wiley & Sons.

Langdon, H. and Cheng, L. (2002) *Collaborating with Interpreters and Translators: A Guide for Communication Disorders Professionals.* Eau Claire, WI: Thinking Publications.

Langdon, H. and Saenz, T. (2016) *Working with Interpreters and Translators: A Guide for Speech Pathologists and Audiologists.* San Diego, CA: Plural Publishing.

Prizant, B. (2016) *Uniquely Human: A Different Way of Seeing Autism.* New York: Simon and Schuster.

Tan, A. (1989) *The Joy Luck Club.* Englewood Cliffs, NJ: Prentice-Hall.

Tan, A. (2007) Mother tongue. In L. Williford and M. Martone (eds) *Touchstone Anthology of Contemporary Creative Nonfiction: Work from 1970 to the Present* (pp. 514–519). New York: Touchstone.

Wallach, G.P. (2011) Peeling the onion of auditory processing disorder: A language/curricular-based perspective. *Language, Speech, and Hearing Services in Schools* 42, 273–285.

8 What Teachers Know About Language

Kimberly C. Feldman, Daniel Ginsberg, and Iris Kirsch

Educational linguistics can have little impact on student learning unless it is effectively conveyed to and applied by teachers in actual classrooms. This chapter presents teachers' perspectives on linguistics in the classroom, from three authors with many years of experience teaching linguistically and culturally diverse learners at the high school level. Currently, Kimberly is a teacher educator, Daniel is an educational linguist and anthropologist, and Iris is a practicing classroom teacher. The vision of linguistically informed education cast by Fillmore and Snow (this volume) captures many of the ideas about language instruction that we have tried to embody in our classrooms over the years. However, we are aware that these approaches to teaching are not practiced in all classrooms, and we recognize the daily barriers faced by teachers and students in a world that does not share our perspective fully. In this chapter, we describe our approaches to linguistically informed teaching, the barriers we have encountered, and our recommendations for teacher education, professional development, and future research.

Valuing Student Language and Identity

In the high school classrooms where she once taught and in her current teacher education classrooms, Kimberly has incorporated an explicit focus on language. She begins this discussion by sharing her own language map—a map of the United States labeled with the words, phrases, and accents of her childhood—and shares stories of *mañana*, *paella*, *lagniappe*, and *gradu*. She shares her pride that her grandfather from Puerto Rico was bilingual and her grandmother born on the bayou was trilingual, and she laments that, although she can understand Spanish and pronounce French words, she speaks neither with much proficiency. She shares how Southern accents feel like home even though she is relieved not to have one because of their negative stereotype. And she shares her shame over feeling that relief. Then her students fill in their own language maps—a U.S. map or a world map. Soon, students begin sharing stories with one another without prompting. Thus begins their exploration of linguistic diversity.

Everything we do related to student language learning is grounded in this conviction: Students' languages and dialects are not only inherently valid and valuable for communication, but also important aspects of their cultural identity. As Fillmore and Snow (this volume) write, "Standard dialects are considered more prestigious than vernacular dialects, but this contrast is a matter of social convention alone. Vernacular dialects are as regular as standard dialects and as useful" (p. 32). We recognize that language prestige is a matter of context—that languages and dialects devalued in school can give students access and prestige in their own communities in a way that academic English cannot. Rather than focusing on student language as a deficit or problem, we focus on the fact that students already have mastery of one or more languages and dialects as a resource for communication and learning. As Fillmore and Snow (this volume) point out, socialization to academic English "is hindered when the language spoken by the children—the language of their families and primary communities—is disrespected in schools" (p. 33). As we provide opportunities for our students to develop academic English, we seek also to provide a safe space for language learning that takes an additive approach to the acquisition of additional languages and dialects. We are not trying to eradicate student language and dialect, but to provide access to additional linguistic resources.

Rather than a specific method for teaching language, we advocate for a mindset grounded in critical language awareness (Fairclough, 2001) that influences how we talk about language, interact with students, grade papers, and provide language instruction. One way that this stance toward language manifests in our classrooms is through open, explicit discussions of standard language ideology (Milroy & Milroy, 2002). We acknowledge the legitimacy of the languages and dialects that students speak as well as the reality that standard language ideologies prevalent in society make it socially and legally acceptable to judge someone based on their language (Adger et al., 2007; Lippi-Green, 2012; Smitherman, 2000). We establish early on that students need to learn standardized English and academic language, not because it is inherently better or more correct, but because it will give them access to opportunities and power that may otherwise be out of reach.

Another way this mindset has manifested in our classrooms is through opportunities for students to engage in linguistic inquiry. One year, Daniel's English as a second language (ESL) IV students learned about several linguistic topics—syntax, child language acquisition, writing systems, translation—which they investigated first by studying unfamiliar languages such as Armenian, American Sign Language, and Cherokee, and then by analyzing their own native languages and giving presentations to their peers (Ginsberg et al., 2011). This unit is one of a number of projects developed by sociolinguists and educators to invite students into the critical study of language and language ideology (Alim, 2009; Christensen, 2000; Godley & Minnici, 2008; Reaser, this volume). As students study their own language the same way they traditionally study standardized English, they come to question the origins and consequences of standard language ideologies in our society and in their communities. And as teachers learn from students and students learn from one another, students' agency is reinforced.

Finally, we demonstrate the importance of student language for learning, communication, and identity in the ways that we include student language in instructional activities. Students are encouraged to use their primary language and dialect when it is needed to communicate with classmates, process new concepts, or write for personal understanding. They are further encouraged to make informed choices about when to use which language and register.

Emphasizing Communication

Fillmore and Snow (this volume) identify five functions in teachers' practice that may be influenced by a more scientific understanding of language, and we see the first, *Teacher as Communicator*, as the foundation that supports the others. It is not possible to educate, evaluate, or socialize students without first establishing good communication. The interaction they cite from Smitherman, in which a student's excited speech is shut down by a teacher's strict insistence on standardized language, is an instructive example. If "Mrs. Jones" recognized her students' language as a valuable form of participation, she would not only provide her students with richer opportunities for language socialization, but also treat them as valued members of the classroom community. Scholarship on second language acquisition and culturally relevant pedagogy affirms that honoring students' home languages will help them acquire other languages and academic content (Delpit, 2009).

According to some theories of second language acquisition (e.g., Krashen, 1981), the sort of correction that Mrs. Jones provides will lead to only minimal improvements in students' knowledge of standardized English. When their "mistakes" are pointed out, students do not learn to speak fluently in a target language or language variety, but only to monitor their speech for "errors." If the goal is for students to acquire a new language or variety, there are techniques for targeted error correction that have been shown to improve grammatical accuracy, but even this approach considers language production to be a pedagogical goal rather than a behavioral norm. If students come to school to learn, then it makes no sense to punish them for not knowing.

When we recognize students' languages and dialects as valid and valuable for communication, and language as a sociocultural practice, not merely a set of decontextualized skills or learning objectives, then a focus on grammatical correctness misses the point: "The primary unit of analysis is *interaction* .... Word play, politeness, language as identity—all these are constitutive of human meaning" (Avineri *et al.*, 2015: 74). Since all interaction takes place within social relationships, establishing and managing the character of those relationships is a crucial responsibility for teachers that necessitates developing the communicative competence to express ourselves effectively, as well as listen to and understand all students. To educate, teachers must be listened to; to evaluate, they must know how to listen; to socialize, they must be trusted. Education is always intercultural communication, as children learn to be students, and students learn to be scholars. If teachers are to build relationships with their students, especially when they do not share a cultural background, then they must begin by recognizing students' language as a tool for communication. We now provide some examples of what that looks like in our approaches to teaching writing.

Supporting Student Writing

Most grade-school students write the way they speak, relying primarily on an informal register in both speech and writing. Teachers who understand the value of all language varieties can help students add new ways of using language for writing. To do that, they need to find a balance between honoring students' language, as reflected in their early writing, and teaching the rules of standardized academic English.

One way to do this is to designate which assignments should be written in academic English and which can be more informal. Iris encourages her high school students to write as they feel moved to at the beginning of the year. She demonstrates that their classroom is a safe space to share ideas however they come out. Whether it is an English class or a creative writing class, she assigns a personal narrative as a major assessment for the first quarter. Similarly, at the beginning of each semester, Kimberly invited her high school students to write letters of introduction in which they expressed their interests and learning preferences in an informal voice with minimal emphasis on grammar and punctuation. In grading these papers, we take note of what students need to work on, but focus primarily on responding to their ideas and praising them heavily for what they do well. These introductory writing assignments give the students a boost of confidence (and a good grade on a major assignment) and they give us a good writing sample early in the year. Throughout the year, we provide opportunities for students to capture their home language in the dialogue of stories and in poetry, and we create opportunities for students to publish their work and see their home languages in print. Honoring their language and voice can be transformative. Sixteen-year-olds have entered our classes saying they hate English and reading, but after having their stories heard and honored, they have gone on to finish reading a novel for the first time in their lives and invest more in other writing assignments than they had previously.

Once our students are willing to write, we can begin critical conversations about the different styles of writing that different assignments call for and how these styles are related to larger social structures. Iris begins the conversation by positing that if there is a desirable engineering job open, it is illegal to refuse to hire applicants based on their race, but it is legal to pass up otherwise perfect candidates because of their grammar. Students indignantly point out that grammar is immaterial in engineering and should not matter, and they often observe that grammatical fanaticism can be used as a stand-in for racism. To contextualize this observation, we engage in consciousness-raising conversations about systemic racism in society based on the myth of white supremacy, the erroneous belief that culture, religion, language, and art from Europe and European-Americans are superior to their counterparts from other cultures. When students recognize linguistic profiling as an expression of systemic racism, some are motivated to master standardized language as an act of resistance.

After having positive writing experiences and engaging in critical conversations about language, our students trust us and have an incentive to begin learning standardized English. With the next academic writing assignment, after drafts and revision, we can teach editing skills. Iris used to tell students to read their papers aloud to see if they sounded right. However, they did sound right to the students— because they wrote in their own voices. Now she tells them to read aloud in their best impression of her voice, which helps them catch more editing opportunities and provides them with a tangible strategy for learning to style shift. We have also found it useful to share quotes from famous authors about revision and editing so that students do not feel that we are telling them they did it wrong, but rather that we would like them to write like professionals. We also make a lot of analogies to perseverance in sports and video games. When a student's grammar deviates significantly from the standard, we pick one or two patterns and focus on them. Once a student is close to being able to maintain a professional register, we focus on finer points.

But the best part—the place where real learning happens—is in one-on-one conferences. For example, Iris sits down with a student when the student is ready, gives her a colored pen, and has her read her paper aloud. As she reads, Iris stops her at various points to discuss why the student's writing is good and, if appropriate, how it could be unclear or confusing. Then they talk about how to communicate the same idea in standardized English without compromising the student's voice. The student decides on the new phrasing herself and writes it on her own paper in colored ink.

After our initial assignments, we steadily increase the percentage of assignments that must be written in standardized English to receive full credit. Personal writing remains informal, so that we are never correcting grammar on someone's journal entry about their father losing his job, for example. We vary the standards for judging student writing based on where each student is on their journey as a writer and on the audience and purpose for each assignment. That way we can keep gently guiding each student to gain proficiency in an academic register while continuing to honor their home dialects.

Acknowledging Barriers

While we and some of our colleagues have found ways to engage in linguistically informed practice, we recognize that not all teachers are doing so. Educational linguists have been attempting for decades to work with teachers on improving their linguistic awareness, but it has proven difficult to add this content to an already overloaded professional knowledge base. Teacher education curricula as well as district professional development schedules are subject to state mandates and local priorities with little room to incorporate new material, especially something like linguistics, which is paradoxically seen by some as both needless technicality and basic common sense. On occasion, sociolinguists have found ways to engage in effective professional development (Mallinson *et al.*, 2011), but for the most part linguistics is not included in teacher learning.

Even when teachers are linguistic experts, there is no guarantee that pedagogy will become linguistically aware and culturally appropriate. Institutions are resistant to change, and schools are no exception; many policies, despite being written with the best intentions, reflect a lack of linguistic awareness in general and reinforce standard language ideology in particular. For example, consider the challenge of providing services for linguistically diverse students with learning disabilities. On the one hand, students of color tend to be overrepresented in special education (Blanchett, 2006), as linguistic and cultural differences are mistaken for cognitive disability. At the same time, we have seen special educators resist assessing struggling English learners until it can be shown that their difficulties are not primarily related to language proficiency. This practice can lead to a procedural impasse, especially when native language assessments are not available, because an undiagnosed learning disability may cause difficulties in language acquisition. In this situation, a linguistically aware teacher can be the student's best advocate (see Cheng, this volume). Being familiar with normative progress in language acquisition and second language learning, we have been able to recognize when students' language did not follow typical learner patterns and bring these concerns to parents and colleagues.

While special education is an issue in which teachers can advocate for their students, standards-based assessments present a different sort of language challenge. Implemented on a large scale, these tests can only be delivered in standardized language since national assessments cannot reasonably be sensitive to all local varieties. While teachers may recognize and value the linguistic diversity that students bring from their home cultures, documents such as the WIDA English Language Development Standards (WIDA, 2012) and the Common Core State Standards (National Governors Association, 2010) are, by definition, a standardizing force. As long as assessments presume proficiency in standardized English, students' native varieties will continue to be viewed as, at best, a tool that teachers can leverage to help students acquire the standard, rather than valuable forms of communication in their own right. Linguistic awareness thus spotlights challenges associated with large-scale standardized testing.

Seeking Solutions

In light of Fillmore and Snow's (this volume) recommendations and the barriers described above, we would like to explore potential recommendations. We agree that increased linguistic education is needed for preservice teachers, which means rethinking the mandated courses that are already in place. We also acknowledge that teacher approaches to language are not likely to change without increased critical consciousness around linguistic prejudice and the racist and classist origins of standard language ideology. Furthermore, we recognize that a purely academic discussion of sociolinguistic principles is unlikely to effect change in teacher practice.

As Fillmore and Snow point out, linguistic concepts can be worked into current course requirements. Most teacher education programs require some sort of foundations-of-education course; if not already included, research related to critical and antiracist pedagogy as well as inequality in education should be incorporated to provide preservice teachers with insight into the underlying racial and socioeconomic factors that impact student access to resources and achievement. These courses can include a critical examination of language education policy and an introduction to the resolution on "Students' Right to their Own Language," composed in 1974 by the Conference on College Composition and Communication (2014) and reaffirmed repeatedly since then by that organization and the National Council of Teachers of English. Sociolinguistic principles and best practices for teaching English learners should also be a significant part of required coursework on differentiating instruction for diverse learners and those with special needs. Finally, many states require at least one literacy course for teaching certification in all grades and content areas. Sociolinguistic principles related to reading and writing can be effectively incorporated into these classes. All of this coursework, however, needs to give preservice teachers opportunities to interact with the concepts in personally meaningful and applicable ways. Engaging in linguistic inquiry in teachers' own communities and field experiences can move these concepts beyond academic theories. Providing preservice teachers with tangible ideas that they can apply in the field, such as those offered by Charity Hudley and Mallinson (2014), will also increase their potential to actually apply these concepts.

Unfortunately, shifts in teacher education are not sufficient to bring about change in pedagogical practice. Increased professional development for in-service teachers is also needed because new teachers are socialized into practice based on their interactions with colleagues early in their careers (Britzman, 2003). If in-service teachers continue to resist linguistically informed practice, new teachers are less likely to engage in practices that are not accepted or encouraged in their schools. Sociolinguistic researchers need to work with curriculum writers and publishers to create resources that support a sociolinguistically informed approach to language learning. Ultimately, curricular materials and tests constrain teacher practice, delimit teacher thinking, and reify standardized English as the one correct form of language for academic instruction and assessment in U.S. schools. Providing teachers with curricula, resources, and alternative forms of assessment could increase teacher confidence in attempting alternative approaches to language instruction in their classrooms.

Finally, we need to acknowledge that teachers must ultimately prepare their students for success in a societal context that continues to engage in language prejudice. While educational linguistics has potential to improve teacher practice and create safe spaces for student language learning, sociolinguists and educators also need to work toward shifting language ideology in society as a whole. Research on critical language awareness and linguistic inquiry in schools seems to focus on classrooms where English learners and speakers of nonstandardized varieties of English predominate. Sociolinguists and educators need to explore these issues with standardized English speakers in predominantly white schools as well, fostering awareness of linguistic privilege and prejudice in all students (see Reaser, this volume). Smitherman (2003) points out that schools are the primary sites where standardized language ideologies are reinforced and reproduced, so they can potentially be the sites where these ideologies are disrupted and shifted.

Conclusion

Fillmore and Snow's (2002) chapter has been influential to many teachers. Our approaches to language instruction illustrate the understanding of student language that we owe in part to them. We acknowledge that more work needs to be done to expand opportunities for teacher candidates, teachers, and the broader society to develop heightened language awareness and increased communicative competence. Yes, preservice teachers need access to these concepts, but concepts alone will not be sufficient to effect change in teacher practice or social norms. We look forward to more collaborations among sociolinguists, students, teachers, administrators, curriculum writers, policymakers, and teacher educators as we continue to find new and better ways to approach language instruction in our classrooms.

References

Adger, C.T., Wolfram, W. and Christian, D. (2007) *Dialects in Schools and Communities.* London/New York: Routledge.

Alim, H.S. (2009) Straight outta Compton, straight aus Munchen: Global linguistic flows, identities, and the politics of language in a global hip hop nation. In H.S. Alim, A. Ibrahim and A. Pennycook (eds) *Global Linguistic Flows: Hip Hop Cultures, Youth Identities, and the Politics of Language* (pp. 1–22). New York: Routledge.

Avineri, N., Johnson, E., Heath, S.B., McCarty, T., Ochs, E., Kremer-Sadlik, T., Blum, S., Zentella, A.C., Rosa, J., Flores, N., Alim, H.S. and Paris, D. (2015) Invited forum: Bridging the "language gap". *Journal of Linguistic Anthropology* 25, 66–86.

Blanchett, W.J. (2006) Disproportionate representation of African American students in special education: Acknowledging the role of white privilege and racism. *Educational Researcher* 35 (6), 24–28.

Britzman, D.P. (2003) *Practice Makes Practice: A Critical Study of Learning to Teach.* Albany, NY: State University of New York Press.

Charity Hudley, A.H. and Mallinson, C. (2014) *We Do Language: English Language Variation in the Secondary English Classroom.* New York: Teachers College Press.

Christensen, L. (2000) *Reading, Writing, and Rising Up: Teaching about Social Justice and the Power of the Written Word.* Milwaukee, WI: Rethinking Schools.

Conference on College Composition and Communication (2014) Students' right to their own language (with bibliography). See http://www.ncte.org/cccc/resources/positions/srtolsummary.

Delpit, L. (2009) Language diversity and learning. In A. Darder, M. Baltodano and R.D. Torres (eds) *The Critical Pedagogy Reader* (2nd edn; pp. 325–337). New York: Routledge.

Fairclough, N. (2001) *Language and Power.* Harlow/New York: Longman.

Fillmore, L.W. and Snow, C.E. (2002) What teachers need to know about language. In C.T. Adger, C.E. Snow and D. Christian (eds.) *What Teachers Need to Know About Language* (pp. 7–54). Washington, DC: Center for Applied Linguistics.

Ginsberg, D., Honda, M. and O'Neil, W. (2011) Looking beyond English: Linguistic inquiry for English language learners. *Language & Linguistics Compass* 5 (5), 249–264.

Godley, A.J. and Minnici, A. (2008) Critical language pedagogy in an urban high school English class. *Urban Education* 43 (3), 319–346.

Krashen, S. (1981) *Second Language Acquisition and Second Language Learning.* Oxford: Pergamon.

Lippi-Green, R. (2012) *English with an Accent: Language, Ideology and Discrimination in the United States.* London/New York: Routledge.

Mallinson, C., Charity Hudley, A., Strickling, L.R. and Figa, M. (2011) A conceptual framework for promoting linguistic and educational change. *Language & Linguistics Compass* 5 (7), 441–453.

Milroy, J. and Milroy, L. (2002) *Authority in Language: Investigating Language Prescription and Standardization* (3rd edn). London: Routledge.

National Governors Association Center for Best Practices and Council of Chief State School Officers (2010) *Common Core State Standards for English Language Arts & Literacy in History/Social Studies, Science and Technical Subjects, Appendix A: Research Supporting Key Elements of the Standards*. Washington, DC: National Governors Association Center for Best Practices and Council of Chief State School Officers.

Smitherman, G. (2000) *Talkin That Talk: Language, Culture, and Education in African America*. New York: Routledge.

Smitherman, G. (2003) The historical struggle for language rights in CCCC. In G. Smitherman and V. Villanueva (eds) *Language Diversity in the Classroom: From Intention to Practice* (pp. 7–39). Carbondale, IL: Southern Illinois University Press.

WIDA (2012) 2012 Amplification of the English Language Development (ELD) Standards. See https://www.wida.us/standards/eld.aspx (accessed 22 February 2017).

9 Language Awareness Programs: Building Students' and Teachers' Sociolinguistic Knowledge

Jeffrey Reaser

In this volume's foundational chapter, Fillmore and Snow note that "Given the diversity of social and cultural backgrounds of the students they serve, educational practitioners need a solid grounding in sociolinguistics and in language behavior across cultures.... Facts about normal language variation are not widely known..." (p. 32). I agree wholeheartedly and endorse the authors' proposed reformulations to teacher education and development so that facts about normal language variation become more widely known and accessible to educators. Lack of knowledge about dialects is a problem not only among teachers, however. In fact, throughout American society, rhetoric surrounding linguistic diversity often frames language variation such that it "is associated with a range of social ills and seen as something that needs to be contained, possibly even something to be fearful of" (Piller, 2016: 2). Changing this widespread ideology requires broad-based efforts, in part because educational policy is influenced by non-teacher shareholders, including parents and politicians. However, given the role that teachers play in the intellectual development of our children and youth, broadly equipping teachers with materials that promote sociolinguistic education may, over time, erode entrenched ideologies. Using such materials in the classroom will also expand teachers' knowledge of sociolinguistics and language variation that will inform their teaching throughout the school day. This chapter examines some efforts to help educators include language awareness in their classrooms. Because the rationale for such programs is made convincingly in the foundational chapter of this volume, no additional theoretical rationale for such work is provided; instead, evidence of the benefits of such programs for students and teachers is presented as a complementary, practical rationale.

Programs that promote awareness about language variation aimed at both school and community audiences have been developed in several areas of the country. The Language and Life Project at NC State University (https://

languageandlife.org/), the West Virginia Dialect Project (http://dialects. english.wvu.edu/), the Wisconsin Englishes Project (http://csumc.wisc. edu/wep/), and other entities created by linguists have adopted proactive, multifaceted approaches to increasing the availability of linguistically accurate information about variation. Each program routinely engages with the public though public lectures, teacher workshops, traditional media interviews, and social media. Some of these programs have also created or contributed to museum exhibits, television documentaries, and general-audience books. Though programs embrace different approaches, at the heart of each of them is spreading the knowledge of a fundamental sociolinguistic principle:

> Like other languages, English has dialects associated with geographical regions and social classes and distinguished by contrasts in their sound system, grammar, and lexicon. Standard dialects are considered more prestigious than vernacular dialects, but this contrast is a matter of social convention alone. Vernacular dialects are as regular as standard dialects and as useful. (Fillmore & Snow, this volume, p. 32)

For the purposes of this chapter, language awareness programs are defined as educational materials that promote an appreciation of language variation through the examination of dialects' and/or language varieties' patterns, histories, and sociocultural significance. These programs may focus on a single dialect or on linguistic variation in a social group, state, region, or country. In general, they include instructional materials (e.g., lesson plans, PowerPoints), audio-visual materials, and student worksheets needed to teach the content. Code-switching programs (e.g., Wheeler & Swords, 2006, 2010), whose primary goal is to build student fluency in the standard code, are not included, even though some of these programs can be broadly interpreted as promoting language awareness. In the following section, some of the approaches for promoting language awareness in K-12 classrooms are detailed. The responses of students and teachers to a few of these programs are then presented, focusing most prominently on responses to the *Voices of North Carolina* language awareness curriculum (Reaser & Wolfram, 2005/2007).

Overview of Language Awareness Materials

Though efforts to provide American teachers with sociolinguistically informed information extend at least as far back as Roger Shuy's (1965) *Social Dialects and Language Learning* and William Labov's (1969) "The Logic of Non-Standard English," in the past decade and a half, there has been a steady increase in the number of language awareness programs. One of the earliest and now longest-running efforts was initiated by

Walt Wolfram in Ocracoke School, on the North Carolina Outer Banks. Since the mid-1990s, Wolfram, his colleagues, and his students have taught a language awareness curriculum annually, first specifically about the local dialect and later expanded to cover language variation across North Carolina. This model of engagement in which linguists and/or their students serve as guest teachers to promote local language awareness has been adopted in many areas, including West Virginia, Washington, South Carolina, New Mexico, and Hawai'i. Though locally impactful, this approach is ultimately difficult to scale: There are simply too many schools and not enough linguists.

The challenges of scalability have been addressed in different ways, most commonly through professional development or by creating materials with enough support so that they can be taught by classroom teachers. One prolonged, successful professional development effort has been undertaken by Anne Charity Hudley and Christine Mallinson. The results of this work, including a number of teacher-created, sociolinguistically informed lessons and activities, are catalogued in their book *We Do Language* (Charity Hudley & Mallinson, 2014). Another approach, using webinars for professional development, is described in Reaser (2016). One set of materials for broad geographical audiences was created for Grades 9–12 (Reaser *et al.*, 2005) to facilitate teachers' use of the documentary, *Do You Speak American?* (MacNeil/Lehrer Productions, 2005). A more recent set of materials supporting a broad geographical audience is based on the rich online and print resources of the *Dictionary of American Regional English* (http://dare.wisc.edu/). *Discovering DARE* was developed to help teachers discuss topics such as the difference between languages and dialects, how language standards evolve, and the role that language (dialects and heritage languages) plays in individual and community identity (Abrams & Stickle, forthcoming).

Some resource books have broad appeal for teachers who wish to promote language awareness in their classrooms. Though not exclusively focused on dialects, they often touch on some topics associated with sociolinguistic awareness. Brown's (2009) *In Other Words* is a workbook that helps students build competence in academic writing and grammar by studying language variation, including some dialect forms like *ain't*. Dean (2008) and Devereaux (2015) both model how teachers can use commonly taught literature as the basis for discussions about dialects that reveal "how dangerously language forms are imbued with values" (Fillmore & Snow, this volume, p. 14). All three books target high school classrooms.

Web-based materials have also been created. Linguist Kristin Denham maintains the *Exploring Language* website (http://www.explorelanguage. org/), which includes lessons for Grades 3–12. Though many lessons explore topics related to standard language and language use in schools (e.g., parts of speech, spelling, punctuation, and clauses), some incorporate information about language or dialect variation.

Because educational decisions, like dialects, are typically locally based, local or state-based curricula may be more desirable to teachers than nationally available materials. The first state-based language awareness curriculum was *Voices of North Carolina: Language and Life from the Appalachians to the Atlantic* (Reaser & Wolfram, 2005/2007), which grew out of the language awareness programs that Wolfram pioneered for Ocracoke School. Unlike previous programs, these materials were designed to be taught by teachers who had no training in sociolinguistics, which would include information about language ideologies, language variation and change, language analysis, and language patterns. Following the success of this project, parallel efforts such as *Voices of the Pacific Northwest* (Pippin & Denham, n.d.), *Appalachian Dialect Unit* (Hazen, n.d.), and *Talking Story about Pidgin* (Higgins, 2010) were created to help teachers share information with students about language variation in local contexts.

Some curricula have examined social dialects, like African American English or Latino English, instead of regional dialects. Sweetland's (2004) language awareness curriculum was built primarily on an investigation of African American English. Designed for elementary students in an urban setting, her curriculum teaches contrastive analysis and examines dialect prejudice. Of particular note is this curriculum's effectiveness for improving student writing. After engaging in the nine-week unit, students in the test group outperformed on formalized writing assessments the students who received the school's traditional Writing Process instruction (Sweetland, 2006). Another project examining social language variation is Henderson's (2016) curriculum for bilingual children in New Mexico. Through the examination of dialects of English, standard Spanish, and local Spanish dialects, bilingual fifth-grade students and their teachers address the goal of understanding that "Acquiring the academic discourse patterns of school is an important part of the educational development of all students, but it is neither necessary nor desirable to promote this ability at the expense of the language patterns children have already mastered and that are essential to functioning effectively in their home communities" (Fillmore & Snow, this volume, p. 16).

Yet another approach is taken by Mary Bucholtz in her School Kids Investigating Language in Life + Society (SKILLS) program in California (http://www.skills.ucsb.edu/). In this program, faculty from the University of California–Santa Barbara support secondary-level student-researchers as they conduct research in communities to answer linguistic questions. Writing about the experience, Bucholtz (2014: 115) notes, "Not only do [students] build on their existing linguistic expertise to acquire important academic skills but they also undergo the transformative experience of appreciating the crucial role of language in their own and others' lives." This experience aligns closely with the goals sketched in the opening chapter to this volume.

Though not exhaustive, this overview of recent language awareness efforts reveals that there are many ways of providing linguistically accurate information and promoting language awareness in classrooms: Linguists can enter classrooms and engage directly with students and teachers; they can engage through web-based professional development; they can train students to become researchers; and they can write books or curricular materials. However, access to quality materials is just one of the challenges in getting more teachers to incorporate language awareness into their classrooms. Teachers are expected to justify their instructional choices, so understanding the impact of such programs is critical to their being adopted more widely.

Some Benefits of Language Awareness Programs

In the opening chapter to this volume, Fillmore and Snow note, "Knowledge about dialect differences can also enrich teaching about language in general, if dialects are treated respectfully and analytically in the classroom" (p. 33). The benefits of classroom-based language awareness programs promise to accomplish this goal and more. While relatively few of the programs described above have been subjected to extensive evaluation, those that have (see, e.g., Henderson, 2016; Reaser, 2006; Sweetland, 2006) find that language awareness has benefits for students and teachers ranging from improving students' scores on standardized writing tests (Sweetland, 2006) to improving their attitudes and knowledge about language variation (Henderson, 2016; Reaser, 2006). And, as discussed later in this section, these programs can also have a substantive effect on instructors who use the materials.

One of the earliest assessments of the effects of a language awareness program was a study of 129 ninth-grade students in North Carolina. The students, spread over five classes and three teachers, were taught the *Voices of North Carolina* language awareness curriculum during a week of their English Language Arts class. A survey conducted before and after teaching the curriculum was used to evaluate students' language attitudes and knowledge. Both versions of the survey contained 20 Likert-type statements that asked students to rate their level of agreement on a four-point scale of "strongly disagree," "disagree," "agree," and "strongly agree." Students were also able to respond "I don't know." The post-curriculum survey included four open-ended response questions.

The following paragraphs overview some changes observed between the pre- and post-curriculum surveys, which illustrate some of the impact that language awareness can have on adolescents' knowledge and attitudes about language variation. A more thorough analysis of these data is found in Reaser (2006). Perhaps the most noteworthy finding is that all 20 Likert-type survey items showed improvement on the post-curriculum survey. A series of paired t-tests found highly significant ($p < 0.02$) changes for 17 of these items. The largest changes were associated with items evaluating students' knowledge about language, including "There are people who do not speak a dialect"; "Everyone should speak Standard English every time they talk"; "Dialects are sloppy forms of English"; and "Dialects do not have patterns" (Reaser, 2006: 115). Survey items more closely tied to language attitudes, such as "Standard English is the best language variety to use at school," also had positive albeit less robust improvements, a difference also reported in Henderson (2016). While it may be discouraging to conclude that attitudes improved less dramatically than knowledge, studies in psychology suggest that knowledge acquisition is a prerequisite to attitudinal changes such as these (e.g., Greenwald & Banaji, 1995).

A second finding of this study is that students seemed to gain confidence in their responses as a result of participating in the curriculum. On average, 12.5% of students responded "I don't know" per item on the pre-curriculum survey. After the unit, these responses decreased to 5.3% (Reaser, 2006: 112). A closer analysis reveals a gender difference: Male and female students began with similar attitudes and knowledge, but female students were more likely than male students to initially respond "I don't know." This gender gap closed by the post-curriculum survey, and females had slightly larger improvements overall in knowledge and attitudes than males, a trend also found by Henderson (2016). Females were also more likely to describe the information as "important to study" in response to one of the open-ended questions on the post-curriculum survey (Reaser, 2006: 137). For example, one female student wrote, "Yes, [it is important to study dialects] because you'll have more respect for people with different dialects and it will give you an open mind. You'll probably judge people on things beside their dialect and the stereotypes attached to that dialect" (Reaser, 2006: 138). Though many male students offered similar sentiments, fully 15% of the male students (compared to 3% of the female students) said it was not important to study dialects. Perhaps surprisingly, this orientation did not seem to affect the impact of the curriculum, as the males who did not value the unit had nearly identical improvements in knowledge and attitudes as the males who did value the unit.

Student responses to the three other open-ended questions provide more evidence as to what students found compelling from their week learning about dialects. In response to the question "What was the most surprising thing that you learned about dialects?," one student wrote: "I learned that a dialect doesn't tell anyone if the person is smart or dumb or anything along those lines" (Reaser, 2006: 131). Another noted, "I learned that dialects aren't sloppy versions of standard English. They follow specific patterns that are logical" (Reaser, 2006: 131). Coding the students' responses by theme revealed that the most surprising thing that students learned was that dialects are rule-governed (34% of the responses). Also reported at high levels was surprise that dialects reflect culture, history, or identity (27%) and that dialects are not related to intelligence or laziness (23%) (Reaser, 2006: 130). These are the sorts of knowledge deemed important in the opening chapter of this volume, which suggests that it is possible to create materials that help teachers promote sociolinguistically informed knowledge even if they themselves have not been previously educated in it.

When asked about why many people have negative attitudes toward dialects, students produced responses that revealed they understood the importance of dialects and the social inequalities that surround vernacular dialects. They found fault with people who "judge too quickly" and assume "If someone can't speak Standard English they are ignorant" (Reaser, 2006: 135). Some noted that their parents held sociolinguistically insensitive or invalid views of dialects, and that many adults would benefit by learning about dialects. Others suggested that sociolinguistic education must begin with young children and be interwoven throughout the public school experience. Overwhelmingly, students suggested that language awareness should be a part of everyone's education.

In addition to finding the information important, the students found the curriculum to be interesting. On an end-of-year course review, more than 90% of the students in two classes (the only two given the survey) noted that this curriculum was their favorite part of the class. Given that students find sociolinguistic information to be educational, important, and engaging, it is hoped that more teachers will be emboldened to seek ways of enriching their students' education by teaching about dialects.

Testimonies from teachers confirm how transformative language awareness can be. Two of the teachers involved with the study described above wrote about their experiences teaching the curriculum. One of them, Ms. Fields-Carey, wrote in part,

> I have found the study of language variations to be a wonderful way to address differences between people, and this aspect of [the dialect curriculum] has been the most valuable part to me and my students.... Discussing bias in relation to language is a non-threatening way to begin thinking and talking about biases in general. (Fields-Carey & Sweat, 2010: 272)

She goes on to describe how the experience transformed her notions about what it means to be an English teacher:

> Through the study of dialects and language differences, my views of what it means to truly teach about the "art of language" has broadened

significantly. I now realize that to understand language is not only to know how to speak and write "standard English" correctly, but also to value the rich tapestry of language in all its forms. (Fields-Carey & Sweat, 2010: 274)

The transformative nature of this knowledge, she notes, is particularly valuable to traditionally at-risk populations. The study of dialect "has proven to be empowering for my minority students. For many of them, this is the first time they have been told in a school setting that their dialect is not 'broken'" (Fields-Carey & Sweat, 2010: 273–274). The other teacher, Ms. Sweat, describes similar transformations in her classroom. She notes, "I began to see the beliefs and prejudices once held by some of my students slowly begin to dissipate" (Fields-Carey & Sweat, 2010: 275). Such programs can effectively sow the seeds of change in both students and teachers.

Conclusion

The benefits of language awareness programs are clear. Students and teachers alike find information about language variation interesting and important, going well beyond merely "enrich[ing] teaching about language in general" (Fillmore & Snow, this volume, p. 33). However, despite the exciting expansion in the number of programs and materials available to educators, there are still too few widely available materials that align with established curricula. And even in locations where such materials exist, schools and teachers have been slow to embrace language awareness for a variety of reasons. Standardized testing requirements dictate many decisions about instructional time and content, which may result in teachers focusing on standard language instruction. But, as Fillmore and Snow note in the opening chapter to this volume, "Too few teachers share or know about their students' cultural and linguistic backgrounds, or understand the challenges inherent in learning to speak or read Standard English" (p. 12). Language awareness programs are one tool for helping teachers better understand their students' linguistic backgrounds and the challenges they face in the classroom, which may just help them on standardized assessments (Sweetland, 2006).

This chapter has offered an overview of some efforts to promote an ideology of language tolerance that complements the important role of academic English in schools while still celebrating language diversity. The hope is that language awareness programs might change the sentiment that while "Our society has had long experience with linguistic diversity ... it has never regarded that diversity as an asset to be valued and protected" (Fillmore & Snow, this volume, p. 23). Celebrating linguistic variation via formal language awareness programs is an essential component for counteracting the devastating effects of widespread ideologies that view vernacular dialects as linguistically inferior to non-vernacular dialects.

There are few facts of life more commonly misunderstood and misrepresented in education and public life than those involving language variation. It is essential for linguists, teacher educators, allied teachers, and policymakers to continue to push for wide-scale efforts to counter this miseducation through every means necessary. Just as we would never tolerate flat-earth teaching in schools, linguists, educators, and the communities they serve should likewise not tolerate scientifically invalid views of language to be perpetuated by our educational institutions.

Links cited

Exploring Language: http://www.explorelanguage.org/

The Language and Life Project at NC State University: https://languageandlife.org/

School Kids Investigating Language in Life + Society (SKILLS): http://www.skills.ucsb.edu/

West Virginia Dialect Project: http://dialects.english.wvu.edu/

Wisconsin Englishes Project: http://csumc.wisc.edu/wep/

References

Abrams, K.D. and Stickle, T. (2017) *Discovering DARE: Lessons from the Dictionary of American Regional English*. Madison, WI: University of Wisconsin. See http://dare.wisc.edu/resources/discovering-dare-curricula (accessed 28 February 2018).

Brown, D.W. (2009) *In Other Words: Lessons on Grammar, Code-Switching, and Academic Writing*. Portsmouth, NH: Heinemann.

Bucholtz, M. (2014) A sociolinguist's vignette: Teaching students the SKILLS of linguistic research. In A.H. Charity Hudley and C. Mallinson (eds) *We Do Language: English Variation in U.S. Schools* (pp. 113–115). New York: Teachers College Press.

Charity Hudley, A.H. and Mallinson, C. (2014) *We Do Language: English Variation in the Secondary English Classroom*. New York: Teachers College Press.

Dean, D. (2008) *Bringing Grammar to Life*. Newark, DE: International Reading Association.

Devereaux, M.D. (2014) *Teaching about Dialect Variations and Language in Secondary English Classrooms: Power, Prestige, and Prejudice*. New York: Routledge.

Fields-Carey, L. and Sweat, S. (2010) Using the *Voices of North Carolina* curriculum. In K. Denham and A. Lobeck (eds) *Linguistics at School: Language Awareness in Primary and Secondary Education* (pp. 272–276). Cambridge: Cambridge University Press.

Greenwald, A.G. and Banaji, M.R. (1995) Implicit social cognition: Attitudes, self-esteem, and stereotypes. *Psychological Review* 102 (1), 4–27.

Hazen, K. (n.d.) *Grades 6–12 Appalachian Dialect Unit*. Morgantown, WV: West Virginia University. See http://dialects.english.wvu.edu/outreach/dialects_in_schools (accessed 28 February 2018).

Henderson, M.H. (2016) Sociolinguistics for kids: A curriculum for bilingual students. Unpublished doctoral dissertation, University of New Mexico.

Higgins, C. (2010) *Talking Story about Pidgin*. Manoa, HI: University of Hawai'i. See http://sls.hawaii.edu/pidgin/ (accessed 28 February 2018).

Labov, W. (1969) The logic of nonstandard English. In J. Alatis (ed.) *20th Annual Round Table. Linguistics and the Teaching of Standard English to Speakers of Other Languages and Dialects* (pp. 1–44). Washington, DC: Georgetown University Press.

MacNeil/Lehrer Productions (2005) Do You Speak American? [Video]. Arlington, VA: Author.

Piller, I. (2016) *Linguistic Diversity and Social Justice: An Introduction to Applied Sociolinguistics*. Oxford: Oxford University Press.

Pippin, D. and Denham, K. (n.d.) Voices of the Pacific Northwest: Language and Life along the Columbia and throughout Cascadia from the 19th Century to the Present. A Curriculum for Middle School Social Studies. See http://www.voicesofthepnw.net/ (accessed 28 February 2018).

Reaser, J. (2006) The effect of dialect awareness on adolescent knowledge and attitudes. Unpublished doctoral dissertation, Duke University.

Reaser, J. (2016) The effectiveness of webinars as a tool for sociolinguistic-based teacher professional development. *American Speech* 91 (2), 235–254.

Reaser, J. and Wolfram, W. (2005/2007) *Voices of North Carolina: Language and Life from the Atlantic to the Appalachians*. Raleigh, NC: NC State University. See https://linguistics.chass.ncsu.edu/thinkanddo/vonc.php (accessed 28 February 2018).

Reaser, J., Adger, C.T. and Hoyle, S. (2005) *High School Curriculum Accompanying PBS's Documentary, Do You Speak American?* Washington, DC: MacNeil-Lehrer Productions. See http://www.pbs.org/speak/education/ (accessed 28 February 2018).

Shuy, R. (1965) *Social Dialects and Language Learning*. Urbana, IL: National Council of Teachers of English.

Sweetland, J. (2004) Sociolinguistic sensitivity in language arts instruction: A literature and writing curriculum for the intermediate grades. Unpublished manuscript, Stanford University.

Sweetland, J. (2006) Teaching writing in the African American classroom: A sociolinguistic approach. Unpublished doctoral dissertation, Stanford University.

Wheeler, R.S. and Swords, R. (2006) *Code-switching: Teaching Standard English in Urban Classrooms*. Urbana, IL: National Council of Teachers of English.

Wheeler, R.S. and Swords, R. (2010) *Code-switching Lessons: Grammar Strategies for Linguistically Diverse Writers, Grades 3–6*. Portsmouth, NH: Firsthand Heinemann.

10 Reflections on "What Teachers Need to Know About Language (2002)"

Kristin Denham and Anne Lobeck

We are linguists who have been teaching undergraduate courses on language and linguistics for over 20 years. We teach in both the English department and the linguistics program, and our students include both linguistics majors and English majors (in literature, creative writing, and elementary and secondary education). A prerequisite of our upper division courses is an introduction to linguistics course.

Here, we report on using Fillmore and Snow's chapter, "What Teachers Need to Know About Language," in the first edition of this book (Adger *et al.*, 2002) in our upper division English classes, addressing in particular how we have used it to familiarize our students, many of whom are preservice teachers, with the role that knowledge of language, and more specifically, knowledge of language based on scientific inquiry, plays in education. We discuss how we also use the text to raise language awareness among students who may not be education majors, including those majoring in English literature, creative writing, and linguistics. We reflect on how teaching with this text has shaped (and continues to shape) some of our programmatic decisions and aspirations, and we hope that our experiences might inspire readers of this new edition.

"What Teachers Need to Know About Language": Fillmore and Snow (2002)

Fillmore and Snow make a very clear case for ways in which all aspects of linguistics contribute positively to teacher preparation, in particular in terms of teaching reading and writing, but also in terms of helping students adapt to the language and culture of school. Their approach strongly contradicts the approach popular in schools over the previous decades to reduce teaching about language in English classrooms: Work on the effects of studying grammar (Harris [1962], popularized in the "Braddock report" [Braddock *et al.*, 1963]) suggested that teaching about language directly—the study of English grammatical terminology—was not only not useful but might even be harmful. The impact of these flawed studies was significant. The Braddock report, Eaton (2003: 79) suggests, "arguably began the decline of grammar instruction in the US." From the 1960s on, direct teaching about language was primarily reduced to mini-lessons in the writing classroom or advice to only "teach grammar in context" (Weaver, 1996, among others). Fillmore and Snow bring the focus back to the many other critical components of language study that are so important for teachers to know and teach. For our university students, who have had little direct study of language in their own schooling and who may also assume such direct study is unimportant, Fillmore and Snow's evidence for the knowledge teachers should have and the crucial role that such knowledge can play out in their classrooms is critical.

Fillmore and Snow (2002) provided convincing and urgent arguments for integrating linguistics into teacher education and also suggested a way to accomplish this through a series of teacher preparation courses. They were aware that the model they were proposing requires systemic change and support from a variety of sources, including administrators, curriculum directors, and others involved in program development and assessment. Their proposals were therefore not aimed narrowly at teachers, but at those involved in designing and implementing teacher education programs. In the new edition, the authors have suggested topics rather than courses, in response to readers of the earlier edition who pointed to the difficulty of expanding an already overflowing curriculum.

In the next sections, we reflect on our own institutional situation, and how we have used the text in our classes to make small but important steps toward the goals that Fillmore and Snow espouse. We then provide an overview of how their text has influenced programmatic changes we have made and hope to still make, inching us ever closer to a model of teacher preparation like the ideal model they propose.

What Everyone Needs to Know

Although we have a strong commitment to integrating linguistics into education, and each of us has worked with in-service teachers on various projects over the years, we, as linguists, do not have the expertise to teach courses on how to teach reading and writing, the cornerstones of K-12 education. Specialists in education teach these courses, and while we are fortunate that at our institution, English Education majors must take some courses in linguistics, our courses do not specifically address ways to practically apply linguistic concepts in the K-12 classroom. But by using "What Teachers Need to Know About Language" in our courses, along with other resources, we raise awareness among all of our students of how knowledge of language is critical in so many aspects of our everyday lives, including, but not limited to, education. We discuss two different courses in which we use this text, as a primary resource in one and as a supplemental resource in the other, to bridge theory and practice.

Linguistics in education

In alternate years, we have the opportunity to teach an upper division elective English course, Linguistics in Education. The course fills up with both English and linguistics majors, some of whom are also enrolled in the English Education program, but many of whom are not. The goals of the course are therefore both to introduce students to the reasons why knowledge of language is so crucial for K-12 teachers and also to provide them with the opportunity to design and pilot mini-lessons on language and to conduct research on applications of linguistics in the classroom.

We begin the course with Fillmore and Snow's chapter; it is very accessible and provides a framework for the larger conversation about educational linguistics. Students are sometimes daunted by the comprehensive overview of systemic change the authors propose, especially when our students do not have access to the kind of teacher preparation program that Fillmore and Snow envision. But, the text certainly provides a model to aspire to and investigate, and it helps to situate their knowledge of language in a broader context.

We supplement "What Teachers Need to Know About Language" with a range of other readings on educational linguistics, including background material on the grammar debates touched on by the infamous Braddock report, along with more current texts that focus primarily on the linguistically diverse classroom: Adger *et al.* (2007); Brown (2009); Charity Hudley and Mallinson (2010, 2013); Reaser and Wolfram (2007); and Wheeler and Swords (2006, 2010). Denham and Lobeck (2005, 2010) examine additional ways that linguistics is integrated into primary and secondary education. We also use some of the growing number of texts targeted at middle and high school teachers that highlight the importance of knowledge about language, integrating discussion of language change and variation into writing pedagogy: Anderson (2005), Benjamin and Oliva (2007), Ehrenworth and Vinton (2005), Schuster (2003), Wilde (2012), among others. Our students use Fillmore and Snow's questions that teachers should be able to answer as a framework for their research and a foundation for their mini-lessons. The breadth of these questions offers a range of options for students with different interests and expertise (these questions from the first edition are slightly revised in this second edition).

- What are the basic units of language?
- What's regular and what isn't?
- How is the lexicon acquired and structured?
- Are vernacular dialects different from "bad English" and if so, how?
- What is academic English?
- Why has the acquisition of English by non-English-speaking children not been more universally successful?
- Why is English spelling so complicated?

- Why do some children have more trouble than others in developing early reading skills?
- Why do students have trouble with structuring narrative and expository writing?
- How should one judge the quality and correctness of a piece of writing?
- What makes a sentence or a text easy or difficult to understand?

The course Linguistics in Education, with "What Teachers Need to Know About Language" as a cornerstone, raises our students' awareness, regardless of their major, of how knowledge of language plays a key role in our schools, and it inspires students, linguistics and English majors alike, to become advocates of educational linguistics. We discuss ways in which knowledge about language is being integrated not only into language arts classrooms, but also into social studies (Denham & Pippin, 2014; Higgins, 2010; Reaser & Wolfram, 2007) and even science (Honda, 1994) classrooms, allowing students to better understand the many benefits of language study, as well as the ways in which its interdisciplinarity is a strength. A few testimonials from students coming out of this class demonstrate the key points that many students take away:

> After taking this class my views on education have changed quite a bit. I realize it is critical to educate *all* students of *all* backgrounds on the diversity of the English language. I think it is really important for children to realize that different dialects are not sub-standard, but simply different, and that they are all rule-governed and systematic. Teaching them where these dialects came from, why they are used, and how they are grammatical in their own way should be a priority for all teachers.

> This course has forced me to look at speakers of other dialects and non-native English speakers in a new way; our discussions about how attitudes about language can affect a child in their learning has helped me to look more closely at my own views of Standard English. I feel that being aware of why students might make the "mistakes" in English that they do based on their home language or dialect is key to helping them feel confident. Embracing the diversity of many languages and dialects will strengthen future generations and hopefully bring them closer together. As a teacher, I plan to encourage this acceptance in my classroom.

> I hadn't ever thought about the place of language study in social studies, but the topics of cultural identity, sovereignty, and civil rights are so intertwined with language. I have gained a real understanding of the links between historical events and language change.

> I finally understand what science really means—that it's not biology or chemistry, but it's a method of inquiry. And it's been so exciting to discover that using language data! Why didn't I know this before?

We also highlight contemporary examples of linguistics in the public sphere—how knowledge about language plays out in policy about bilingualism in schools, Official English legislation, and spelling reform. Students use tools of linguistic analysis to question and challenge social attitudes about language and how those attitudes contribute to language subordination and discrimination. Even for those students who do not plan to be teachers, the material in this class and in the Fillmore and Snow chapter highlight the importance of language study for all students and for all teachers—and, therefore, for all of us—thereby strengthening the case for extensive language study that Fillmore and Snow are rightfully calling for.

The structure of English

All of our teaching involves touching on some of the aspects of knowledge about language that Fillmore and Snow argue are fundamentally important for teachers, and we believe that such knowledge is fundamentally important for all students. They write, "Teachers need to have access to basic information about language for the same reasons that any educated member of society should know something about language" (Fillmore & Snow, this volume, p. 22). We very much agree, and using their chapter is therefore useful beyond teacher education. For these reasons, that chapter can be used as a resource in almost any linguistics course (and almost any education course, for that matter).

We regularly teach a 400-level course on English descriptive grammar, The Structure of English. The course is required of secondary English Education majors, but it is also populated with students of linguistics, English literature, and creative writing. This course focuses primarily on the syntactic structure of English and on the tools of linguistic inquiry we use to analyze that structure. Another component of the course focuses on how the grammatical structure of English changes over time and varies over space. Therefore, this course provides vital information and tools critical to teaching about language, along with knowledge about language that, as Fillmore and Snow assert, an educated member of society should know.

In this course, we supplement the more technical study of grammatical structure with a series of readings and discussions that illustrate a variety of ways in which a deeper understanding of language and how it works can lead us to investigate and challenge linguistic misinformation and discrimination, which often shape our institutions, policies, and ideologies. In addition to "What Teachers Need to Know About Language," we include resources that deepen students' understanding of linguistic diversity and language change from different vantage points. Students explore the origins of prescriptive grammatical rules and notions of language authority and

Standard English (Curzan, 2002; Evans, 2011; Milroy & Milroy, 1999), the politics of teaching bidialectalism (O'Neil, 1972), and code-switching (Young, 2009; Young & Martinez, 2011; Wheeler & Swords, 2006), how social media affects language change, and more. Other readings we have used include Alim and Smitherman (2012), Mufwene *et al.* (1998), Smitherman (2000), and Sweetland (2005). Each of these readings, like "What Teachers Need to Know About Language," situates our students' knowledge of language in a broader social and institutional context and provides them with tools to challenge myths and stereotypes about language that are vital not only for teachers but also for all students.

Looking Forward

One of the strengths of Fillmore and Snow's chapter in the earlier volume and in this one as well is that it is both unapologetic and uncompromising in its demand for changes based on existing and clearly documented needs. Their vision for teacher preparation requires integrating linguistics (and linguists) into education in a comprehensive and focused way. Disciplinary boundaries, however, may well inhibit this integration; while linguists are becoming more and more involved in education, many of us are faculty members in other departments and programs, such as English, World Languages, or Teaching English to Speakers of Other Languages (TESOL). In order to achieve the kind of comprehensive curricular reform that Fillmore and Snow propose, we must find ways to cross boundaries and use the interdisciplinarity of linguistics as strength. Better integration between those who teach linguistics and those who teach in teacher preparation programs and schools of education is critical. To that end, we have reached out on our own campus to those who teach in our separate College of Education and have found common ground in the TESOL program and with our colleagues who teach within the new English Language Learners endorsement program. This endorsement for teachers can accompany any content area certification. A course on English Linguistics for Pre-K-12 is required, as well as courses on second language acquisition and bilingualism. So change is afoot. We are also in discussion with colleagues across our campus about developing a graduate program in Educational Linguistics to produce teachers who have the kind of knowledge about language and linguistics that Fillmore and Snow advocate for, and to encourage experts on language to become involved in educational policy.

Fillmore and Snow do set a high bar, but it's one we should strive for. That a second edition of *What Teachers Need to Know About Language* has appeared some 15 years after the first, with an updated but equally urgent message, is energizing; and it encourages us to remind ourselves not only of the progress we have made, but also of all the work that remains to be done. All of what Fillmore and Snow write about is still relevant and extremely important. Their work has inspired us to keep at it, and their arguments can be used to convince others of the importance of linguistics in education. We hope not only that other linguists and teacher educators read and teach this text, but that others will as well; we all need to recognize and continue to work for systemic change.

References

Adger, C.T., Snow, C.E. and Christian, D. (eds) (2002) *What Teachers Need to Know About Language*. Washington, DC/McHenry, IL: Center for Applied Linguistics and Delta Systems, Inc.

Adger, C.T., Wolfram, W. and Christian, D. (2007) *Dialects in Schools and Communities*. Mahwah, NJ: Lawrence Erlbaum Associates.

Alim, H.S. and Smitherman, G. (2012) *Articulate While Black: Barack Obama, Language, and Race in the U.S.* Oxford: Oxford University Press.

Anderson, J. (2005) *Mechanically Inclined: Building Grammar, Usage, and Style into Writer's Workshop*. Portland, ME: Stenhouse Publishers.

Benjamin, A. with Oliva, T. (2007) *Engaging Grammar: Practical Advice for Real Classrooms*. Urbana, IL: National Council of Teachers of English.

Braddock, R., Lloyd-Jones, R. and Schoer, L. (1963) *Research in Written Composition*. Urbana, IL: National Council of Teachers of English.

Brown, D.W. (2009) *In Other Words: Lessons on Grammar, Code-Switching, and Academic Writing*. Portsmouth, NH: Heinemann.

Charity Hudley, A.H. and Mallinson, C. (2010) *Understanding Language Variation in U.S. Schools*. New York: Teachers College Press.

Charity Hudley, A.H. and Mallinson, C. (2013) *We Do Language: English Language Variation in the Secondary English Classroom*. New York: Teachers College Press.

Curzan, A. (2002) Teaching the politics of Standard English. *Journal of English Linguistics* 30 (4), 339–352.

Denham, K. and Lobeck, A. (eds) (2005) *Language in the Schools: Integrating Linguistic Knowledge into K-12 Education*. Mahwah, NJ: Lawrence Erlbaum Associates.

Denham, K. and Lobeck, A. (eds) (2010) *Linguistics at School: Language Awareness in Primary and Secondary Education*. New York: Cambridge University Press.

Denham, K. and Pippin, D. (2014) *Voices of the Pacific Northwest: A Curriculum for Middle School Social Studies*. See http://www.voicesofthepnw.net/.

Eaton, A. (2003) The effectiveness of two methods of correcting formal error. *Business Communication Quarterly* 66 (2), 79–83.

Ehrenworth, M. and Vinton, V. (2005) *The Power of Grammar: Unconventional Approaches to the Conventions of Language*. Portsmouth, NH: Heinemann.

Evans, A. (2011) Beyond grammar: Linguistics in language and writing courses. *Pedagogy: Critical Approaches to Teaching Literature, Language, Composition, and Culture* 11 (2), 285–300.

Fillmore, L.W. and Snow, C.E. (2002) What teachers need to know about language. In C. Adger, C.E. Snow and D. Christian (eds) *What Teachers Need to Know About Language* (pp. 7–54). Washington, DC/McHenry, IL: Center for Applied Linguistics/ Delta Systems, Inc.

Harris, R. (1962) An experimental inquiry into the functions and value of formal grammar in the teaching of English, with special reference to the teaching of correct written English to children aged twelve to fourteen. Doctoral dissertation, University of London.

Higgins, C. (2010) *Talking Story about Pidgin*. See sls.hawaii.edu/Pidgin.

Honda, M. (1994) Linguistic inquiry in the science classroom: 'It is science, but it's not like a science problem in a book'. *MIT Occasional Papers in Linguistics* 6. Cambridge MA: MITWPL.

Milroy, J. and Milroy, L. (1999) *Authority in Language: Investigating Standard English* (3rd edn). London/New York: Routledge.

Mufwene, S.S., Rickford, J.R., Bailey, G. and Baugh, J. (1998) *African-American English: Structure, History, and Use.* New York: Routledge.

O'Neil, W. (1972) The politics of bidialectalism. *College English* 33 (4), 433–438.

Reaser, J. and Wolfram, W. (2007) *Voices of North Carolina Dialect Awareness Curriculum.* See http://www.ncsu.edu/linguistics/research_dialecteducation.php.

Schuster, E. (2003) *Breaking the Rules: Liberating Writers through Innovative Grammar Instruction.* Portsmouth, NH: Heinemann.

Smitherman, G. (2000) *Talkin' that Talk: Language, Culture, and Education in African America.* London: Routledge.

Sweetland, J. (2005) Evaluation of contextualized contrastive analysis in language arts instruction. Doctoral dissertation, Stanford University.

Weaver, C. (1996) *Teaching Grammar in Context.* Portsmouth, NH: Heinemann.

Wheeler, R. and Swords, R. (2006) *Teaching Standard English in Urban Classrooms.* Champaign/Urbana, IL: NCTE Press.

Wheeler, R. and Swords, R. (2010) *Code-Switching: Grammar Strategies for Linguistically Diverse Writers.* Portsmouth, NH: Heinemann.

Wilde, S. (2012) *Funner Grammar: Fresh Ways to Teach Usage, Language, and Writing Conventions.* Portsmouth, NH: Heinemann.

Young, V.A. (2009) 'Nah, We Straight': An argument against code switching. *JAC* 29 (1-2), 49–76.

Young, V.A. and Martinez, A.Y. (2011) *Code-Meshing as World English: Pedagogy, Policy, Performance.* Champaign/Urbana, IL: National Council of Teachers of English.

11 What Teacher Educators Need to Know About Language and Language Learners: The Power of a Faculty Learning Community

Elizabeth R. Howard and Thomas H. Levine

I never learned how to explain a concept, like plant growth, in terms that they [emergent bilinguals] would understand, because I don't speak Spanish.... And I don't know how to teach them things that I can't explain. I only speak English.

I don't do a whole lot of differentiation. It's mostly just, because there are no required modifications for my ESL students, it's mostly just checking in with them, making sure they understand what's going on and that they're clear. I have one student that has a translator, so I allow him to have that out.

These quotes from former participants in the University of Connecticut's teacher education program highlight some challenges and misperceptions of preservice teachers, and provide evidence of gaps in their preparation for working effectively with emergent bilinguals. Several years ago, through exit surveys completed after graduation, our preservice teachers voiced the concern that they were not adequately prepared to meet the needs of these students in their classrooms. In Connecticut, as in the country as a whole, there has been considerable growth in the English language learner population in recent years (NCES, 2015); Connecticut has also struggled with a sizeable and persistent achievement gap for this group as evidenced through lower standardized achievement test scores and lower graduate rates (Megan, 2014). Our preservice teachers' feelings of being unprepared were not surprising, despite the requirement of a three-credit diversity course in the teacher education course sequence. Many teacher education faculty themselves felt inadequately prepared to support preservice teachers in their learning about emergent bilinguals. They saw that a stand-alone course did not help preservice teachers to integrate supports for emergent bilinguals into their core teaching practices, particularly since the diversity course is offered after the completion of methods courses and student teaching. Thus motivated by feedback from our graduates, shifting demographics, and growing recognition among our teacher education faculty of our own need for professional learning in this area, we initiated Project PREPARE-ELLs (Preparing Responsive Educators who Promote Access and Realize Excellence with English Language Learners), a multi-year faculty learning community designed to increase the capacity of the teacher education faculty to adequately prepare preservice teachers to work effectively with emergent bilinguals. The following sections provide a conceptual framework for this type of faculty development work, describe our activities and the impact of the project, and provide recommendations to others who may be interested in initiating a similar project.

A Conceptual Framework for Faculty Development

The "Framework for Teacher Learning" developed by the National Academy of Education's Preparing Teachers for a Changing World project (Darling-Hammond & Bransford, 2005) posits that effective teachers must develop specific understandings, practices, and dispositions, all of which are underpinned by visions of what is possible. In the case of preparation to work with emergent bilinguals, these components are highly aligned with the issues raised by Fillmore and Snow in the opening chapter and discussed in greater detail in subsequent chapters of this volume, as well as with the seven characteristics of linguistically responsive educators put forth by Lucas and Villegas (2010, 2011). For example, specific understandings that preservice teachers require to work effectively with bilingual students include knowledge about second language development, discipline-specific academic language demands, and the cultural and linguistic practices of the community. Additionally, preservice teachers need to develop pedagogical practices for helping emergent bilinguals access the core curriculum and develop language and literacy skills at the same time. The third component, dispositions, addresses the importance of valuing linguistic and cultural diversity and seeing students' home experiences as assets rather than limitations. Underlying the knowledge, practices, and dispositions of preservice teachers are the visions of what is possible, which can motivate teachers to question status quo classroom practices (Cochran-Smith, 1991) and continue to reinvent themselves and improve their teaching.

Drawing on this framework for preservice teachers' learning, we put forth a parallel framework for teacher educators (Figure 11.1) that builds

Teacher Educators' Understandings	Teacher Educators' Practices	Teacher Educators' Dispositions
• K-12 teacher understandings • K-12 teacher practices • K-12 teacher dispositions		
Vision (seeing what is possible and desirable in teacher preparation courses, i.e., content area methods courses, clinical seminars assessment, etc.)		

Figure 11.1 Conceptualizing what teacher educators must develop to improve teacher preparation for work with emergent bilinguals. Reprinted with permission of Taylor and Francis Group LLC Books, from *Preparing Classroom Teachers to Succeed with Second Language Learners: Lessons from a Faculty Learning Community*, T. H. Levine, E. R. Howard, and D. M. Moss (2014); permission conveyed through Copyright Clearance Center, Inc.

on the original by embedding the needed understandings, practices, and dispositions for preservice teachers into the needed understandings of teacher educators. Further, teacher educators must also develop appropriate practices for weaving relevant information about emergent bilinguals into their already packed courses, along with the disposition that this is a worthwhile use of limited class time. Like K-12 teachers, teacher educators' work can be improved if they have a vision of how possible and desirable it is to address linguistic and cultural diversity in their own courses and across the program.

Models of Faculty Development

Guided by this conceptual framework, we developed a faculty learning community to improve teacher preparation for linguistic diversity. This work built upon many previous years of faculty support activities designed to promote learning about the needs and strengths of emergent bilinguals among teacher educators and preservice teachers. These prior activities align with approaches described in the literature, and they form what we consider to be a developmental progression of models of faculty development (Figure 11.2). The first model constitutes a form of pull-in support, where teacher educators invite colleagues with expertise in the education of emergent bilinguals into the methods class to provide a guest lecture (Meskill, 2005). While this approach is generally easy to implement, it does not allow for sustained learning or systemic course change on the part of the teacher educators, nor does it enable preservice teachers to integrate the learning about emergent bilinguals with their other learning in the course.

Individual mentoring is another approach, in which a faculty member with expertise in the education of emergent bilinguals works extensively with colleagues to help them modify course content and pedagogical practices. Millie Gort, our former colleague who pioneered efforts at UConn to infuse the needs of emergent bilinguals throughout the teacher education program, provided ongoing mentoring of this type to two teacher

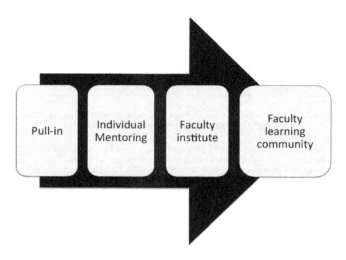

Figure 11.2 Conceptualizing a developmental progression: Four additive models of promoting teacher educators' capacity to prepare teachers for linguistic diversity. Reprinted with permission of Taylor and Francis Group LLC Books, from *Preparing Classroom Teachers to Succeed with Second Language Learners: Lessons from a Faculty Learning Community*, T. H. Levine, E. R. Howard, and D. M. Moss (2014); permission conveyed through Copyright Clearance Center, Inc.

educators at our institution (Gort *et al.*, 2010). This approach is effective in that it promotes the knowledge development of participating faculty and enables them to weave key understandings and skills more deeply into the content and assignments of their course; however, it is time-consuming and difficult to scale up to an entire teacher education faculty.

A third model is the faculty institute, in which a group of faculty members meets regularly to discuss shared readings and consider course modifications (Brisk, 2008; Costa *et al.*, 2005). This approach, like the individual mentoring approach, has the benefit of being sustained and is therefore more likely to result in learning on the part of the teacher educators. However, the extent to which this learning gets translated into practice may be limited, particularly if the activities focus primarily on reading. This was our experience at the University of Connecticut. In our first year, we joined three other teacher education faculty members in a reading group initiated by Millie Gort. While we enjoyed our shared reading and discussion about topics such as effective pedagogical practices for emergent bilinguals or the challenges of academic language, we found that these activities had only a modest impact on curriculum and instruction.

To address the limitations of these approaches, we initiated and co-facilitated a fourth model, a faculty learning community. Over a period of three years, 18 teacher education faculty met monthly to share practices, discuss readings, and carry out joint research. This group included all four clinical faculty members, all major subject area methods instructors with the exception of one who was transitioning to another role in the teacher education program, and two additional instructors of teacher education courses. We were fortunate to secure internal funding from the university as well as through Teachers for a New Era (an initiative of the Carnegie Foundation), and these funds enabled us to support a graduate student, fund speakers, pay small stipends to participating teachers, and provide lunch during monthly meetings. Through this intentional community of practice (Lave & Wenger, 1996; Wenger, 1998), we sought to create new understandings, dispositions, and access to specific practices for K-12 education, along with visions of possible practice in teacher preparation. We also sought to help each other examine our individual practices, thus creating opportunities for building a sense of joint enterprise focused on common aims and experiences.

Sustaining a Faculty Learning Community

Purpose

We believe that effective faculty learning communities engage participants in three interdependent and mutually reinforcing activities: ongoing professional development (see "knowledge for practice" in Cochran-Smith & Lytle, 1999); sharing of—and learning from—instructional practices (Curry, 2008; McDonald *et al.*, 2003); and research (Fairbanks & Lagrone, 2008; Hubbard & Power, 1999).

To that end, we opened each monthly meeting by restating our purpose: *We, in Project PREPARE-ELLs, are engaged in learning together so that we can improve our individual courses and our program's efforts to prepare teachers for linguistic and cultural diversity. Beyond our professional development work, we explore the problems and progress in our courses so that we learn from each other, and engage in research aimed at helping ourselves and others improve our practice.* Continually reminding ourselves of our purpose helped us to retain focus and make ongoing progress through the many years and multiple activities of the project.

Activities

Ongoing professional development

Faculty members are often both comfortable with and good at learning from reading books and articles, and attending lectures and workshops. Though we sought to go beyond the limits of such learning to promote action, we did use these traditional means of building knowledge as one part of our learning community. For example, we launched our project with an intensive one-week summer professional development program that involved a four-day training workshop on the Sheltered Instruction Observation Protocol (SIOP) (Echevarria *et al.*, 2012) with Deborah Short, one of the creators of the instrument and its corresponding instructional approach, as well as a one-day workshop on academic language with María Brisk, an expert on the language and literacy development of bilingual students. This week of professional development built on the previous readings and discussions of the subgroup involved in our prior years of meeting as a reading group (faculty institute), and also laid the groundwork for the initial activities of the faculty learning community. At the end of the first year, we read "What Teachers Need to Know About Language" (Fillmore & Snow, 2000) and deepened our understanding of the text through a discussion with Catherine Snow during our last meeting. Prior to our discussion with Catherine, we met in the morning to engage in a jigsaw reading of the article, with one expert group focusing on oral language and the other on written language. We then formed pairs with one member from each expert group to share information across sections, and ended by coming together to brainstorm questions for our meeting with Catherine that afternoon.

In our second year, we brought culture to the forefront, reading and talking about funds of knowledge (Gonzalez *et al.*, 2005) as well as sociocritical literacy, language hybridity, and the third space (Gutiérrez, 2008; Gutiérrez *et al.*, 1999), while also continuing our exploration of academic language through the work of Schleppegrell and colleagues (e.g., Schleppegrell & O'Hallaron, 2011). We were once again fortunate to complement our reading with a discussion with one of the authors by inviting Kris Gutiérrez to join us while she was on campus for a language symposium.

Sharing of practice through protocol-guided conversations

To help us move our new understandings into practice and work through resulting problems and dilemmas, we used protocols that specify the nature and length of various phases of a conversation with the aim of promoting more robust outcomes. The National School Reform Faculty has developed protocols like those we used to give educators both permission and a gentle push to make their teaching challenges visible, to actively address aspects of others' teaching even if they are not used to playing this role, and to use limited time together very efficiently (for more information, see McDonald *et al.*, 2003 or Levine *et al.*, 2014). Our protocol-guided presentations and discussions included topics such as alternative ways of framing information about emergent bilinguals, linguistic registers and domain-specific academic language, the relationship between language and culture, and the challenge of finding time to address the topic of emergent bilinguals in already packed methods courses. We had no prior history of publicly revealing the things we were struggling to do; protocols gave us explicit permission and held us accountable to present problems with specificity, to offer help and critique, and thus to engage in kinds of conversation, problem-solving, and collective learning that are otherwise counter-normative among K-12 teachers (and, in our experience, professors).

Conducting and disseminating research

Incorporating research into our faculty learning community was essential, not only because of the information it gave us about project impact and future steps, but also because scholarly activity weighs heavily in decisions regarding promotion and tenure, and thus provides a strong incentive for faculty participation. We carried out research focusing both on our own efforts as teacher educators and on the impact on preservice teachers. We encouraged participating faculty to conduct and disseminate their own individual research related to project goals, and also dedicated meeting time in our first two years to discussing the content and structure of an edited book (Levine *et al.*, 2014), which we co-authored during our third year, using our meeting time as a writers' workshop. The book incorporated both research that individual faculty had carried out independently in their courses and research that we had carried out systematically as a group, including repeated administrations of a self-efficacy measure for preservice teachers, student teacher observations in the classroom, and reflective memos and interviews with participating faculty.

Impact

Impact on faculty

All participating faculty made changes to their practice in the form of course modifications, such as adding readings and/or modifying course projects or class discussions to help preservice teachers consider how the topic at hand might relate to emergent bilinguals. All teacher educators further agreed to introduce and establish the importance of including language objectives along with content objectives when engaged in K-12 lesson planning. This had been a primary take away of the four-day SIOP training and was easily positioned as a key change that all faculty could make to increase preservice teachers' thinking about language demands within their disciplines. Participation in the faculty learning community impacted many individuals' independent research activities, and all members co-authored chapters of the book exploring aspects of our work and its impact on our preservice teachers' self-efficacy and enacted practices.

Impact on students

The impact on preservice teachers was assessed both at the course level and at the program level. At the course level, individual teacher educators determined how they wanted to explore the impact on preservice teachers. For example, our English methods instructor partnered with our former colleague Millie Gort to explore how two of her preservice teachers responded to aspects of her methods course addressing emergent bilinguals, and to see how any of this teaching did and did not show up in student teaching (Glenn & Gort, 2014). At the program level, we created the Teacher of English Language Learners Self-Efficacy Scale (TELLSES), a self-reported measure of knowledge and practices related to the effective education of emergent bilinguals, such as teachers' familiarity with effective pedagogical strategies and the extent to which they implement those strategies. We administered the TELLSES to successive cohorts of preservice teachers at multiple points over a four-year period to help us gauge potential changes in self-efficacy within and across cohorts, and found statistically significant mean gains in self-efficacy, along with progressively higher mean scores at the time of program completion. We also observed a sample of preservice teachers as they delivered a lesson during their student teaching and rated the lesson using the SIOP (Echevarria *et al.*, 2012). We found ample evidence of student teachers incorporating language objectives, a practice few of us had promoted before our work in Project PREPARE-ELLs. Of the seven SIOP features that we saw student teachers enacting least often, five related to supporting language development and comprehension, thus reinforcing the concerns expressed by Fillmore and Snow (this volume) and suggesting the next steps for our work.

Recommendations

For those who may be interested in forming a faculty learning community at their own institution, we offer a few recommendations:

1. *Start simply and simply start.* Starting on a smaller scale with individual mentoring and a faculty institute (reading group) eventually made our larger faculty learning community possible.
2. *Determine and respond to the unique needs, motivations, and incentives for faculty in your own context.* In our case, preservice teacher feedback on exit surveys provided a compelling rationale for faculty to make time to improve our program, and the focus on research and dissemination provided a strong incentive, given the professional expectations at a Research 1 university.
3. *Develop routines and activities that promote sustainability over time by addressing faculty needs and promoting action.* This practice is important, since accountability and results will likely generate even more commitment and action. To that end, we set a monthly meeting schedule and held to it for several years, while recognizing that not every faculty member would be able to attend every meeting. Additionally, relying on a consistent protocol to guide presentations and discussions helped us to move forward.

"What Teachers Need to Know About Language" (Fillmore & Snow, 2000) and the similar chapter in the first edition of this book (Adger *et al.*, 2002) have sparked much thinking and discussion in our program and in the field in general, and we are grateful to have the updated version in this volume as a resource. Our case makes clear that it is possible, desirable, and even joyful for faculty to learn together and engage in change that positively impacts preservice teacher preparation for linguistic diversity.

References

Adger, C.T., Snow, C.E. and Christian, D. (eds) (2002) *What Teachers Need to Know About Language.* McHenry, IL/Washington, DC: Delta Systems/Center for Applied Linguistics.

Brisk, M.E. (2008) Program and faculty transformation: Enhancing teacher preparation. In M.E. Brisk (ed.) *Language, Culture, and Community in Teacher Education* (pp. 249–266). Mahwah, NJ: Lawrence Erlbaum Associates.

Cochran-Smith, M. (1991) Learning to teach against the grain. *Harvard Educational Review* 61 (3), 279.

Cochran-Smith, M. and Lytle, S. (1999) Relationships of knowledge and practice: Teacher learning in communities. In I.N. Ashgar and D.P. Pearson (eds) *Review of Research in Education: Vol. 24* (pp. 249–305). Washington, DC: American Educational Research Association.

Costa, J., McPhil, G., Smith, J. and Brisk, M.E. (2005) Faculty first: The challenge of infusing the teacher education curriculum with scholarship on English language learners. *Journal of Teacher Education* 56 (2), 104–118.

Curry, M.W. (2008) Critical friends groups: The possibilities and limitations embedded in teacher professional communities aimed at instructional improvement and school reform. *Teachers College Record* 114 (4), 733–774.

Darling-Hammond, L. and Bransford, J. (eds) (2005) *Preparing Teachers for a Changing World: What Teachers Should Learn and Be Able to Do.* San Francisco, CA: Jossey-Bass.

Echevarria, J.J., Vogt, M.J. and Short, D.J. (2012) *Making Content Comprehensible for English Learners: The SIOP Model* (4th edn). Boston, MA: Pearson.

Fairbanks, C.M. and Lagrone, D. (2006) Learning together: Constructing knowledge in a teacher research group. *Teacher Education Quarterly* 33 (3), 7–25.

Fillmore, L.W. and Snow, C.E. (2000) *What Teachers Need to Know About Language.* Washington, DC: ERIC Clearinghouse on Languages and Linguistics.

Glenn, W.J. and Gort, M. (2014) Preservice teachers' evolving knowledge and practice toward linguistically- and culturally-responsive pedagogy. In T.H. Levine, E.R. Howard and D.M. Moss (eds) *Preparing Classroom Teachers to Succeed with Second Language Learners: Lessons from a Faculty Learning Community* (pp. 190–218). New York: Routledge.

Gonzalez, N., Moll, L.C. and Amanti, C. (2005) *Funds of Knowledge: Theorizing Practices in Households, Communities, and Classrooms.* Mahwah, NJ: Lawrence Erlbaum Associates.

Gort, M., Glenn, W.J. and Settlage, J. (2010) Toward culturally and linguistically responsive teacher education: The impact of a faculty learning community on two teacher educators. In T. Lucas (ed.) *Preparing Teachers for Linguistically Diverse Classrooms: A Resource for Teacher Educators* (pp. 178–194). New York: Routledge/Taylor & Francis.

Gutiérrez, K.D. (2008) Developing a sociocritical literacy in the third space. *Reading Research Quarterly* 43 (2), 148–164.

Gutiérrez, K.D., Baquedano-López, P. and Tejeda, C. (1999) Rethinking diversity: Hybridity and hybrid language practices in the third space. *Mind, Culture, and Activity* 6 (4), 286–303.

Hubbard, R.S. and Power, B.M. (1999) *Living the Questions: A Guide for Teacher-Researchers*. Portland, ME: Stenhouse Publishers.

Lave, J. and Wenger, E. (1996) *Situated Learning: Legitimate Peripheral Participation*. New York: Cambridge University Press.

Levine, T.H., Howard, E.R. and Gort, M. (2014) Recruiting and organizing learning among busy faculty members. In T.H. Levine, E.R. Howard and D.M. Moss (eds) *Preparing Classroom Teachers to Succeed with Second Language Learners: Lessons from a Faculty Learning Community* (pp. 37–62). New York: Routledge.

Levine, T.H., Howard, E.R. and Moss, D.M. (2014) *Preparing Classroom Teachers to Succeed with Second Language Learners: Lessons from a Faculty Learning Community*. New York: Routledge.

Lucas, T. and Villegas, A.M. (2010) The missing piece in teacher education: The preparation of linguistically responsive teachers. *National Society for the Study of Education* 109 (2), 297–318.

Lucas, T. and Villegas, A.M. (2011) A framework for preparing linguistically responsive teachers. In T. Lucas (ed.) *Teacher Preparation for Linguistically Diverse Classrooms: A Resource for Teacher Educators* (pp. 55–72). New York: Taylor & Francis.

McDonald, J., Mohr, N., Dichter, A. and McDonald, E. (2003) *The Power of Protocols: An Educator's Guide to Better Practice*. New York: Teachers College Press.

Megan, K. (2014) Connecticut's students learning English perform poorly compared to nation. *The Hartford Courant*. See http://www.courant.com/news/connecticut/hc-connecticut-bilingual-education-1220-20141225-story.html#page=1 (accessed 15 January 2017).

Meskill, C. (2005) Infusing English language learner issues throughout professional educator curricula: The Training All Teachers project. *Teachers College Record* 107 (4), 739–756.

National Center for Education Statistics (NCES) (2015) *The Condition of Education 2015 (NCES 2015-144), English Language Learners*. Washington, DC: U.S. Department of Education.

Schleppegrell, M.J. and O'Hallaron, C.L. (2011) Teaching academic language in L2 secondary settings. *Annual Review of Applied Linguistics* 31, 3–18.

Wenger, E. (1998) *Communities of Practice: Learning, Meaning, and Identity*. New York: Cambridge University Press.

Index

Made in the USA
Las Vegas, NV
19 August 2021